THE POEMS OF CATULLUS

GUY LEE is a Fellow of St John's College, Cambridge. He has translated numerous Latin texts including works by Ovid, Virgil, Tibillus, and Persius. His translation of Propertius' *Poems* is published in Oxford World's Classics.

OXFORD WORLD'S CLASSICS

═══

The Poems of Catullus

═══

*Edited and translated
with an Introduction and Notes by*

GUY LEE

OXFORD
UNIVERSITY PRESS

OXFORD
UNIVERSITY PRESS

Great Clarendon Street, Oxford OX2 6DP

Oxford University Press is a department of the University of Oxford.
It furthers the University's objective of excellence in research, scholarship,
and education by publishing worldwide in

Oxford New York

Athens Auckland Bangkok Bogotá Buenos Aires Calcutta
Cape Town Chennai Dar es Salaam Delhi Florence Hong Kong Istanbul
Karachi Kuala Lumpur Madrid Melbourne Mexico City Mumbai
Nairobi Paris São Paulo Singapore Taipei Tokyo Toronto Warsaw

with associated companies in Berlin Ibadan

Oxford is a registered trade mark of Oxford University Press
in the UK and in certain other countries

Published in the United States
by Oxford University Press Inc., New York

First published 1990
First published as a World's Classics paperback 1991
Reissued as an Oxford World's Classics paperback 1998

British Library Cataloguing in Publication Data

Data available

Library of Congress Cataloging in Publication Data

Catullus, Gaius Valerius.
[Works. English. 1991]
The Poems of Catullus/edited with introduction, translation,
and brief notes by Guy Lee.
p. cm.—(Oxford world's classics)
Originally published: 1990.
Includes bibliographical references.
1. Catullus, Gaius Valerius—Translations, English.
I. Lee, Guy. II. Title. III. Series.
[PA6275.E5L44 1991] 874'.01—dc20 90–49440

ISBN 0-19-283587-4

7 9 10 8 6

Printed in Great Britain by
Clays Ltd, St Ives plc

ACKNOWLEDGEMENTS

Apart from all my obligations to past and present scholars who have worked on Catullus, and in particular to Professor George Goold of Yale University for the challenge and the assistance provided by his edition and translation of Catullus, I owe a special debt of thanks to two friends: first to Professor Wendell Clausen of Harvard University who read the introduction and the translation and whose learning and encouragement have been of the greatest help; secondly to Professor Kenneth Quinn, formerly of University College, Toronto, who read the translation and the notes and whose objections and hesitations have made me think again and again about more points than I can remember.

St John's College   A. G. L.
Cambridge
June 1989

CONTENTS

INTRODUCTION

The Text

Catullus could easily have suffered the fate of his friends
Calvus and Cinna: his work, like theirs, could have
survived only fractionally in a few wretched fragments
quoted by grammarians. But the Gods decreed otherwise
—or, quite simply, we were lucky. One manuscript of his
poems, complete save for some dozen gaps of a line or
more, was brought to his home town of Verona 'from a
far frontier', as an epigram attached to it recorded, at the
very beginning of the fourteenth century. This MS is
known as *V*, short for *codex Veronensis*. A little later a
copy of *V* was made, perhaps by Petrarch; this copy is
known as *X*. *V* and *X* have both disappeared, but about
1375 another copy of *V* was made; this is now in the
Bodleian Library at Oxford and is therefore known as *O*
(*codex Oxoniensis*). Soon after, two copies were made of
X; the first, *G* (*codex Sangermanensis*), is now in the
Bibliothèque Nationale in Paris, the second, *R* (*codex
Romanus*), is in the Vatican Library. It is on these three
late fourteenth-century MSS, *O*, *G*, and *R*, representing
their lost common ancestor *V*, that our text of Catullus is
based. Admittedly for Poem LXII there is also available
an important ninth-century witness, *T* (*codex Thuaneus*),
like *G* now in the Bibliothèque Nationale. This, however,
while providing correct readings against *V* in several
places, after verse 32 exhibits the same lacuna as *V* and
must therefore descend from a common ancestor. All
other existing MSS of Catullus (over 140) are descended
from *OGR*, and their variant readings are of interest only
as conjectures.

Yeats in his well-known poem *The Scholars*, which
might more reasonably be called *The Pedants*, imagines
how horrified those 'old, learned, respectable bald heads'
would be if they could meet the real Catullus. In fact

Catullus would have been far more horrified could he
have seen the state of his text at the beginning of the
fourteenth century, some 1350 years after his death.
With tongue in cheek he had hoped that his *nugae* or
trifles would last for more than one generation; but,
gratified as he would be to know that they had lasted by
then for forty-five generations, he could hardly have
foreseen the frightful metamorphosis they had undergone.
It was not simply that his original spelling had disappeared,
though a few traces of that do remain, e.g. II. 6 *karum* and
lubet, XLVI. 3 *aureis*, LXII. 60 *aequom*. That is a fate to
be suffered eventually by all authors who have the
misfortune to become classics; Chaucer, Shakespeare,
Milton, have all endured it; it is comparable to the
cleaning and re-touching that great pictures are put
through. No, the real shock for Catullus would have been
the plague of error visible in *V*. Catullus had written
Cinna est Gaius, and *V* gave *cuma est grauis*; he had
written *expuli tussim*, and *V* gave *expulsus sim*; he had
written *non si illam rarae*, and *V* gave *nos illa mare*. And
so the long tale of error goes on throughout the whole of
his book.

Goold has estimated that *V* must have contained no
fewer than a thousand mistakes. Most of them were
minor and fairly easy to correct, e.g. VII. 5 *oradum* and 11
euriosi for *oraclum* and *curiosi*. Some, like the three
examples given above, were more difficult and took
longer to emend; thus *Cinna est Gaius* is dated to 1473,
expuli tussim to 1495, *non si illam rarae* to 1502. A very
beautiful correction was that of Scaliger in 1577, who
saw that the original behind *V*'s *sed michi ante labello* at
LXI. 213 must have been *semihiante labello*. It needed
Bentley in 1697 to divine that *V*'s *sanguinis* at LXVI. 91
should be *unguinis*, and Housman in 1889 to see that the
vulgate reading *Emathiae tutamen opis, carissime nato*
at LXIV. 324 should be *Emathiae tutamen, Opis carissime
nato*.

So down the centuries Yeats's despised Scholars have
gradually purified the text of Catullus and brought it ever
nearer to what its author intended. In textual criticism,

at any rate, one can forget about the so-called 'Intentional Fallacy', that pathetic modern academic belief which takes for granted the perfection of the text one happens to be reading and maintains that one has no right to talk about the author's intention, because his intention is precisely the words on the page in front of one's eyes—words, incidentally, of which any interpretation is believed to be as true as any other. To return to Yeats's poem: amusing as it may be, it is hardly fair to The Scholars, for despite baldness, respectability, coughing in ink, and wearing out the carpet, it is to them that we owe the text of Catullus; were it not for them there would be no Catullus to read.

The Latin text here offered to the reader was produced with the help of printed editions (mainly those of Baehrens, Ellis, Postgate, Palmer, Merrill, Kroll, Mynors, Quinn, Thomson, and Goold) and of commentaries (mainly those of Baehrens, Ellis, Merrill, Kroll, Fordyce, Quinn, and Ferguson). Interested readers will find recorded in Appendix A the differences between this text and the Oxford Classical Text of Sir Roger Mynors, whose lectures on textual criticism the translator was privileged to attend and to whom he chiefly owes such understanding as he has of that indispensable art and would-be science.

The Collection

The text of Catullus handed on to us by The Scholars apparently consists of 116 poems—apparently, because the modern numeration jumps from XVII to XXI and Poems XVIII, XIX, and XX are missing. This is because the French humanist Antoine Muret or Muretus (to give him his Latin name) inserted at this point in his edition of Catullus (1554) three epigrams to Priapus which he regarded as the work of Catullus, though only the first is certainly a genuine fragment. These three insertions were ejected by Lachmann from his edition of 1829, though he retained the now anomalous numeration.

Despite these omissions the total number of poems can remain 116 if we regard those numbered II B, XIV B, and LXXVIII B as fragments of three separate poems and LVIII B as part of LV. But it must be confessed that this last idea is not very likely and that the grand total of poems is more probably 117.

When we look at the composition of the book comprising these 117 poems, we find that it divides most obviously into three parts: I–LX, short poems in various metres but excluding hexameters and elegiac couplets (this part is commonly referred to as the *Polymetra* or *Polymetrics*); LXI–LXVIII, long poems (LXV being a covering letter for LXVI); LXIX–CXVI, epigrams in elegiac couplets.

But LXV–LXVIII are also written in elegiac couplets, and further consideration will show that they belong more naturally with the elegiac epigrams that follow than with the preceding group of four long poems. In the first place, at LXV. 12 Catullus announces that he 'will always sing songs saddened' by his brother's death. Now the elegiac couplet was regarded as a mournful metre (*flebilis Elegia*, Ovid, *Amores* III. ix. 3) and the line can thus introduce the whole series of elegiac poems that follows. Secondly at LXV. 16 we find a reference to the translation of a poem by the Alexandrian Greek poet Callimachus; similarly, at the beginning of CXVI, the last poem of all, we again find a reference to the translation of Callimachus, thus rounding off this third section of Catullus' book with an echo of its beginning.

The second section begins with a long wedding song connected with the first section by the use of a metre already found there in Poem XXXIV, the hymn to Diana. Then comes a shorter wedding song in hexameters, followed by a rather longer poem in galliambics. The last poem in this section, LXIV, is an epyllion or miniature epic on the wedding of Peleus and Thetis, which ends with the song the Three Fates sang (in hexameters, of course, but with refrain) at the wedding and with a final comment by the poet explaining why the Gods in his day no longer come down from heaven and appear to men.

Here again there is a rounding off of the section by a reference back to its beginning: the wedding song of the Fates with refrain is parallel to Poem LXII, also with refrain and in hexameters, and the topic of divine epiphany occurs at the beginning of LXI, a beginning which, technically speaking, is a kletic or invocatory hymn to the God of Marriage, entreating him to appear.

We may note in conclusion, first, that each of these three sections of Catullus' book contains at the start a reference to a Muse or the Muses: thus I. 9 addresses her in the guise of *patrona Virgo*, LXI. 2 refers to her as Urania, and LXV. 2 laments the poet's separation from the *doctae Virgines*; secondly, that each section begins with an allusion to Callimachus: thus I. 1 *lepidum* is an etymological reference to the Greek word describing the type of verse he approved, LXI. 2 Urania as Hymen's mother comes from his *Aetia*, LXV. 16 introduces the translation of his *Coma Berenices* that follows in LXVI; thirdly, that each section is of a convenient length for a papyrus roll of poetry—I–LX 848 lines, LXI–LXIV 795 lines, LXV–CXVI 646 lines.

In view of these facts it seems a reasonable assumption that Catullus' present book appeared in three papyrus rolls or *libelli*. A poetic papyrus roll containing 2290 lines and more seems very unlikely if Catullus, an admirer of Callimachus, published his work himself, for Callimachus is well known to have said that 'A big book is big trouble'. Besides, Catullus introduced the first *libellus* as *lepidum nouum libellum*, referring to the collection it contained as *nugae*, words which better suit a collection of 848 lines of short poems or epigrams in various metres than a collection of more than 2290 lines containing *inter alia* a poem of 408 epic hexameters. And that Catullus did himself arrange his work for publication seems likely from the cross-references already mentioned, cross-references which an editor of the poet's work is unlikely to have spotted and made use of in his editorial arrangement.

The likelihood that Catullus was his own editor is increased by the arrangement of the *Polymetra*. Wiseman has shown that they are arranged roughly in three cycles or groups. First comes the Lesbia group, II–XIV. After this the fragmentary poem XIV B warns the reader that something more shocking is to follow and introduces the homosexual group of Juventius poems, XV–XXVI. Then comes XXVII, another prelude, calling for stronger wine and introducing a group of political and personal lampoons, XXVIII–LX. It is also worth noting that the two poems in the rare sapphic metre are placed ten poems from the beginning of the first _libellus_ (starting not with the dedication to Cornelius Nepos but with _Passer, deliciae_ and counting II B as a separate poem) and ten poems from its end (counting LVIII B as a separate poem). The three _libelli_ would be joined together in one _liber_ when the codex or bound volume of parchment leaves came into fashion, replacing the papyrus roll.

But, it is objected, why do ancient grammarians never refer to Book I, II, or III of Catullus? Surely the absence of any mention by them of Books means that Catullus' work was from the very beginning one large collection of poems? This conclusion does not necessarily follow. Ancient grammarians often refer to authors by name and quotation simply, without giving Book numbers or even the name of the work. As regards Catullus this minimal form of reference would be perfectly suitable, because the metre of the quotation would nearly always enable one to know the _libellus_. Thus anything in elegiacs must come from Book III, anything in hexameters from Book II, anything in any other metre (save galliambics and the glyconics of LXI) from Book I.

Catullus the Epigrammatist

Because he writes short and intense poems about his own feelings, modern readers tend to think of Catullus as a lyric poet, and indeed Jerome in his _Chronica_ (late fourth century A.D.) actually describes him as 'the lyric writer' (_scriptor lyricus_). But Jerome's reason for this label is likely to have been the purely formal one that Catullus used lyric metres (hendecasyllables, sapphics, asclepiads, glyconics, etc.) in Poems I–LX, LXI, and LXIII. Earlier in antiquity, however, he was classed not as a lyric poet but as an epigrammatist.

Martial, epigrammatist *par excellence*, regards him as the originator of the genre in Latin (see the prose preface prefixed to Book I of his *Epigrams*) despite the fact that Ennius and Lucilius had written epigrams in the second century B.C., and that Calvus and Cinna are known from their Fragments to have written epigrams in the same metres as Catullus. Martial also regards him as the greatest Latin exponent of the genre and his own highest ambition is to be placed second on the list of epigrammatists after Catullus (Martial x. 78. 14–16). It should be noted that he counts as epigrams not only the elegiac couplets of LXIX–CXVI but also the hendecasyllables and iambics of I–LX, because he refers to Catullus' *Passer* as his model, meaning by that word the whole *libellus* whose first word it is (Martial IV. 14), and because he himself includes hendecasyllables and iambics among his elegiacs. Theocritus had done the same in the third century B.C., and Martial's contemporary the younger Pliny states that his own collection of hendecasyllables could just as well be called epigrams (Pliny, *Epistles* IV. 14). Like Catullus, Martial refers to his verse as *nugae* and to his books as *libelli*.

Martial counts epigram as lowest in the hierarchy of literary genres (XII. 94) and specifically states that its subject matter is everyday life: *agnoscat mores Vita legatque suos*, 'Let Life (here) recognize and read about her own behaviour' (VIII. 3). According to him epigram as a genre exhibits two features which are likely to repel the squeamish: first, personal abuse; secondly, coarse language (*lasciua uerborum ueritas, id est epigrammaton lingua*, Martial I, *praefatio*). As regards the first of these Martial emphasizes that he himself never attacks real people, even the humblest, in this differing from his predecessors, who did not hesitate to name real names and even great ones (*nomina magna sed et uera*, ibid.). But as regards the second characteristic, obscenity, he writes: 'I would apologize for it if I were the first to use it, but Catullus, Marsus, Pedo, Gaetulicus, all write like that—so does any epigrammatist worth reading.'

In fact what Martial says about epigram helps us a great deal in understanding Catullus. Admittedly Catullus never mentions the word, but no one would wish to deny that LXIX–CXVI in elegiacs are epigrams; as Ross has shown they carry on a tradition started in Latin by Ennius. As regards I–LX the word _iambi_, 'iambics', crops up three times: at XXXVI. 5 and LIV. 6 in hendecasyllables, and at XL. 2 in scazons or limping iambics. Now _iambi_, ever since the Greek poet Archilochus' first use of the metre, was a technical term for invective verse, and invective verse, as Martial, tells us, is characteristic of epigram.

Even the reader who reckons that he knows Catullus' work well will be surprised, when he actually counts up its total of obscene and/or abusive poems, to find out how very many of them there are. It is in fact much quicker to list those that contain no element of obscenity or abuse. Among the _Polymetra_ they total a mere twenty, viz. I–V, VII–IX, XIII, XXXI, XXXIV–V, XLV–VI, XLVIII–LI, LV, LVIII B—that is, about one third. Among the elegiac epigrams the proportion is even smaller—ten out of forty-nine, viz. LXXXV–VII, XCII, XCVI, C–CII, CVII, CIX, and that includes one (LXXXVI) which could reasonably be counted out on the ground that it is insulting to Quintia. It must therefore be admitted that at least two-thirds of Catullus' epigrams are such as either 'do not lend themselves to comment in English' (as Fordyce archly observes) or exemplify personal abuse or are at the same time obscene and abusive.

We do not know whether Catullus was the first to lace his collection of epigrams with so much invective or whether this element was already present in similar proportion in contemporary Greek collections. On the one hand, ribald Fescennine verses were a characteristic Latin thing, and Rome was notorious as _maledica ciuitas_, 'a slanderous community' (Cicero, _Pro Flacco_ 48); on the other hand, Catullus is well known as a *doctus poeta* or scholar-poet (Martial calls him *doctus* on several occasions) and was well acquainted with Greek literature, as is shown by his translations from Sappho and Callimachus, his knowledge of Greek epigram, and his not unlikely connection with the Hellenistic poet Parthenius, a connection emphasized by Clausen. It is perhaps unlikely then that as first of the Latin epigrammatists (if we can trust Martial) naturalizing a fresh Greek genre in Latin he would have departed far from contemporary Greek precedent. This of course is not to deny that his individual epigrams are different from their Greek counterparts, as may clearly be seen by a comparison of Philodemus' invitation to Piso (*Greek Anthology* XI. 44) with Catullus' invitation to Fabullus (XIII), or Meleager's grave-epigram for Heliodora (*Greek Anthology* VII. 476) with Catullus' for his brother (CI). The Latin epigrams have an immediacy and a closeness to the spoken language that is lacking in the more ornate and 'poetical' Greek.

Moreover Catullus attacks real people, his contemporaries, including the great and powerful among them. As Martial implies, this is the cardinal difference between the two poets, and it reflects first of all their different social standing, and secondly the different political state of their times. Both poets were provincials, but Catullus came from a rich and influential family in the neighbourhood of Verona. He had the entrée to high society in Rome and like the satirist Lucilius in the previous century could afford to throw his weight about. Besides, he wrote in the turbulent times of the First Triumvirate of Pompey, Caesar, and Crassus, times marked by political in-fighting, electoral corruption, and public disorder, when he and his friends could safely play the part of a Roman Republican *Private Eye*. Martial, on the other hand, an impoverished citizen from Bilbilis in Spain, lived under the tyranny of the Emperor Domitian, when political freedom was minimal and one had to watch out for informers. Private need and the temper of the times demanded that he attack lay figures. He could count himself lucky to get away with obscenity under an emperor so insistent on public propriety that he buried alive a Chief Vestal Virgin found guilty of immorality.

Catullus' Life and Poetry

A recent book on Catullus begins with this statement: 'We do not know very much about the life of Catullus'. It is true that we have very few hard facts about his life. External information is limited to a mere three or four items. Jerome in his *Chronica* tells us that Catullus was born at Verona in 87 B.C. and died in his thirtieth year in 57 B.C. Unfortunately the second date must be wrong, because there are poems of Catullus which allude to events after 57 B.C.; thus CXIII refers to Pompey's second consulship, which fell in 55 B.C., and XI refers to Caesar's invasion of Britain, which took place in the autumn of that same year. It is customary to suppose that Jerome is right about Catullus' age and to choose 54 B.C. as the date of his death and therefore 84 B.C. for his birth.

The one reasonably certain date in his life is that of his service in the province of Bithynia on the staff of the governor Memmius from 57 to the spring of 56 B.C. This date depends on a letter of Cicero to his brother Quintus (*Ad Quintum Fratrem* I. 2. 16) from which we gather that Memmius is praetor designate for 58 B.C. It was normal for a praetor to remain in Rome during his year of office and in the following year to proceed to a provincial governorship. If Memmius did the regular thing, then the earliest datable poem of Catullus is XLVI, written in the spring of 56 B.C. when he was on the point of returning from Bithynia to Italy via some of the famous cities of Asia Minor.

Suetonius in his *Life of Julius Caesar* tells us that Catullus' father was accustomed to entertain Caesar, which means that he must have been one of the local aristocrats of Cisalpine Gaul, certainly a land-owner, with a villa on the peninsula of Sirmione on Lake Garda (XXXI), and Wiseman further suggests (1985, 100) that he was a businessman with interests in Spain and Asia

Minor. In the same place Suetonius records that Catullus'
verses about Mamurra (presumably XXIX and LVII) were
recognized by Caesar as having brought an indelible
stigma on himself, but that when the poet 'made amends'
he invited him to dinner.

Apuleius tells us in his *Apologia*, some two hundred
years after Catullus' death, the real name of the woman
Catullus calls Lesbia, and incidentally provides us with
Catullus' own praenomen or first name, thus: 'Gaius
Catullus used the name Lesbia for Clodia'. Apuleius will
have got this information from Suetonius' *De Poetis*,
who in his turn, according to Wiseman (1969, 51–2), will
have had it from Julius Hyginus, librarian of the Palatine
Library in the time of Augustus, interested in modern
poetry (*uatum studiose nouorum*, Ovid, *Tristia* III. 14. 7)
and author of *De Vita Rebusque Illustrium Virorum*.

Apart from these few items of information from other
writers we are dependent on Catullus' own poems for
knowledge of his life. And in fact they tell us a great deal
about the man and the sort of life he led. Indeed it would
be true to say that we know more about Catullus from
his poetry than about any other classical poet, with the
exception of Horace and Ovid. This is because two thirds
of his work are concerned with actual moments, incidents,
and personalities in his life. Virtually all his epigrams
(I–LX as well as LXIX–CXVI) are concerned with his
emotional reactions to other people, his contemporaries.
Even those epigrams concerned with places (XXXI Sirmio,
and XLIV his farm), things (IV his yacht, and XLII his
hendecasyllables), or animals (II–III Lesbia's sparrow)
personify their subjects and treat them as human beings.
His reactions to other people usually arise from some
event in his daily life: he welcomes a friend back from
military service in Spain, records an incident that
happened to him in the Forum to his disadvantage, taxes
an acquaintance with the theft of some table-napkins,
invites a friend to a rather special dinner, complains
about being given an anthology of bad poetry at the
Saturnalia, advises a friend on a poem, consoles Calvus
on the death of his beloved Quintilia, celebrates the

publication of Cinna's long-meditated miniature epic.
After reading some hundred epigrams about the poet's
friends and enemies and about things that happened to
him, one feels one knows a good deal about him and the
sort of life he led.

Of course this is not to say that one can take
everything he tells us as gospel truth. In literary studies,
as in most other departments of life, fashion swings from
one grotesque extreme to the other. In the nineteenth
century many scholars took poetic statements as too
literally related to real life; in the twentieth many have
believed that poetry has no relation at all to life but exists
in a self-referential vacuum or a self-contained world of
literary allusion. One even meets sceptics who do not
believe that Catullus' Lesbia really existed; and if they
mean that the picture of Lesbia one gets from Catullus'
poems about her is not a faithful representation of the
historical character to whom the pseudonym refers, then
they may well be right. But if they mean that the
pseudonym is purely fictitious and refers to no historical
character at all, then on the evidence of Apuleius they are
wrong.

Unfortunately Latin has no definite or indefinite
article, so we cannot know whether Apuleius meant 'a
Clodia' or '*the* Clodia'. For us '*the* Clodia' is the Clodia
attacked by Cicero in his speech *Pro Caelio*, the Clodia
married to Metellus Celer, who held the praetorship in
63 B.C. and the governorship of Cisalpine Gaul (Catullus'
homeland) the year after that, the Clodia notorious for
her sexual licence, who was even rumoured to have
murdered her husband Metellus by poison. But this
Clodia had two sisters, who also spelt their patrician
name of Claudia in the plebeian way as Clodia, following
the example of their brother Publius Clodius Pulcher,
Cicero's enemy. Which of these three Clodias was
Catullus' Lesbia?

Since the Renaissance most scholars have favoured
Metellus' Clodia: she was married, which fits with
Catullus' admission that the affair was adulterous (LXVIII.
143–6); she also had an affair with Marcus Caelius Rufus,

which fits with Catullus' reference to 'our Lesbia' in Poem LVIII addressed to a Caelius, and with his bitter complaint in Poem LXXVII that a Rufus has betrayed him; she would have known Catullus from at least 60 B.C. until 55 when he finally breaks with her in Poem XI, a space of time which can reasonably allow the affair to be described in Poem LXXVI as 'a long love'.

The opponents of this identification, however, point out that the first datable poem of Catullus is XLVI, written just before his return from Bithynia in 56 B.C., and that all the other datable poems (IV, XXXI, XI, XXIX, XLV, LII, LV, LXXXIV, and CXIII) are later than that. Besides, Catullus' Caelius, according to Poem C, is a native of Verona, whereas Cicero's Caelius Rufus came from the Ancona area; moreover Catullus' Rufus apparently suffers from gout and halitosis (LXIX and LXXI), whereas Cicero's Caelius Rufus was an elegant young man about town.

There is also an important metrical argument to be taken into account. It has been pointed out that Catullus' treatment of the first two syllables, or base, of the hendecasyllabic line varies according to an odd pattern. In the 263 hendecasyllables of Poems II–XXVI there are only four exceptions to spondaic base (two long syllables), viz. II. 4, III. 12 and 17, VII. 2. On the other hand, in the 279 hendecasyllables of Poems XXVIII–LX there are sixty-three exceptions—thirty-three with iambic base (short, long) and thirty with trochaic (long, short) Now Poem I, the dedication to Cornelius Nepos, which we can reasonably suppose to have been written last of all the poems I–LX, has one iambic and three trochaic bases in its ten lines. Professor Otto Skutsch (1969, 38) has therefore inferred that Catullus began by sticking strictly to the rule that a hendecasyllable should begin with a spondee, but as time went on gradually relaxed this restriction.

His argument provides a possible means of the relative dating of the hendecasyllabic poems, which Wiseman develops. The earliest datable poem, XLVI, has spondaic bases only. So too Poem X (a long one of 34 lines), Poem V (clearly an early Lesbia poem), and Poems VI, IX, XII–XV, XVI (clearly later than V, to which it refers), XXI, XXIII–XXIV, XXVI, XXVIII, XLIII (again a Lesbia poem), XLVIII, LVI–LVII. In short, according to Wiseman, we have no reason to suppose that any Lesbia poem is earlier than 56 B.C., and therefore Catullus' Lesbia cannot have been Metellus' Clodia, because she was a widow at that time, whereas Catullus states that he was committing adultery.

Fascinating as it may be, the question of Lesbia's identity is not of great importance to Catullus' readers. Its answer leaves his poetry unaffected. He has not wished his readers to identify Lesbia and that is why he has given her a pseudonym. Why did he choose that particular pseudonym? It means literally 'the woman from Lesbos', as *Andria*, the title of Terence's play, means 'the woman from Andros'. Curiously enough a Lesbia occurs in the cast of Terence's *Andria*—as a midwife. This is not an allusion likely to have occurred to Catullus! Professor Wendell Clausen, who made these points in conversation, believes that Catullus' original readers would have taken Lesbia as the name of a Greek courtesan from Lesbos and that that was what Catullus meant them to do. After all, if we can believe Apuleius, Catullus was committing adultery with an aristocratic Roman lady. He would not wish her to be publicly dishonoured, and moreover he himself disapproved of adultery (LXI. 97–9). Presumably he first used the pseudonym in Poem LI, his adaptation of Sappho's famous poem, where it would have most point (for Sappho was a native of Lesbos); so the knowledgeable reader of that poem would naturally associate the name with Sappho. But while this is probably so, Catullus has deliberately concealed the connection from the reader by placing Poem LI late in his *libellus* and introducing the name without any Sapphic associations in Poem V. From its appearance in this poem, in which love is implicitly contrasted with money as the thing worth living for, the reader would guess that Lesbia was a Greek courtesan and Catullus not wholly serious. But, on reading on in the collection, he would be amazed by the number, the content, and the quality of the Lesbia poems; for as Lyne (1980, 60) has pointed out 'Catullus is the first ancient poet to treat a love-affair . . . in depth, in a related collection of mutually deepening poems', and this treatment was an inspiration to many later poets.

The importance of Lesbia in the life of Catullus, however, must not incline us to underestimate the importance to him of his poet-friends, in particular of Gaius Licinius Calvus (XIV, L, LIII, XCVI) and Gaius Helvius Cinna (X, XCV, CXIII). In XCV Catullus greets the publication of Cinna's brief epic narrative poem, or epyllion, the *Zmyrna*, just as the Alexandrian Greek poet Callimachus had greeted the publication of Aratus' *Phaenomena*, and by the epigram's balanced structure and allusive content, by its attack on the verbosity of Hortensius and the *Annals* of Volusius, and by its praise of the small-scale and its scorn for the popular taste for the orotund, indicates, indeed exemplifies, the sort of poetry approved by Cinna and himself. That was the poetry Callimachus had championed, concentrated, subtle, erudite, and allusive, the result of much thought and revision. What Cinna had produced was an epyllion in the contemporary Greek manner, re-telling an out-of-the-way legend about a daughter who fell in love with her own father, deceived him into intercourse, was changed into a myrrh tree, and in due time split open to bear a son, Adonis. Cinna's bizarre *Zmyrna* (this spelling represents the Greek pronunciation of *Smyrna*) is lost, save for two hexameters, but we have Catullus' own epyllion, LXIV, as first surviving representative of this new genre in Latin poetry.

No less revealing in its different way than XCV is Catullus' epigram L to Calvus, recording how they spent an evening together drinking and improvising *versiculi* in various metres. Key words here are *ludere*, *delicati*, *lepor*, and *facetiae*, pointing to light verse, sophistication and impropriety, elegance, wit, and humour. In fact the poem is intended to be an object-lesson in precisely these qualities, its impropriety being the barefaced declaration of love for Calvus in a poem designed to be read by the

general public (Calvus himself would not need to be
given the information provided in lines 1–6). The word
versiculi (for which Quinn in his commentary proposes
the translation 'epigrams') has already appeared in XVI,
another indecent mock-serious piece, indeed a poetic
manifesto intended to justify the sort of poetry that
Poems I–LX represent—and one would not need to
justify an already existing type of verse.

Catullus' work mirrors himself, and in it we can
clearly see that Lesbia, his brother, his friends, and poetry
were the four loves of his life. If he has a message, it can
be summed up (surprisingly enough) in that untranslatable
word *pietas*, with its overtones of duty, devotion, respect,
and even pity. He claims to have shown this quality in
his love for Lesbia (LXXVI. 2), in his relationship with an
unnamed friend (LXXIII. 2), and in his vocation as a poet
(XVI. 5). Although the word does not occur in the famous
farewell to his brother (CI), that grave-epigram is un-
mistakably an embodiment of *pietas*. But his *pietas* goes
unrewarded. Lesbia spurns him; his friend betrays him;
he loses his brother. His ideal lives on, however, in the
mind of Virgil, whose own observation of life may well
have combined with his reading of Catullus to extend its
scope into the domain of public life and to make it the
key to the character of his epic hero Aeneas.

The Translation

Since 1945 at least sixteen English translations of
Catullus have appeared in print, the freest (of those
published in this country) that of Peter Whigham in The
Penguin Classics series, the liveliest (and most shocking!)
that of Frederic Raphael and Kenneth McLeish, the
most reliable that of George Goold. Faced with such
competition, what is the latest translator of Catullus to
do?

There is surely no point in adding yet another to the
number of free translations or paraphrases, however
lively. In these days, thanks to our experts in education,

there is quite enough 'creativity' about, and perhaps what is most needed in a world of hype is a little honesty. So the translator's best course will be to follow the example of George Goold and, if possible, produce a version as reliable but even more compressed.

Consider the first two lines of Catullus' dedication to Cornelius Nepos:

> *Cui dono lepidum nouum libellum*
> *arida modo pumice expolitum?*

Whigham renders:

> *To whom should I present this*
> *little book so carefully polished . . .*

Raphael and McLeish:

> *Who's to be offered my brand-new slim volume*
> *Slickly polished with dry-as-dust pumice-stone?*

Goold:

> *To whom do I give my pretty new book,*
> *freshly polished with dry pumice?*

The present translator:

> *Whom do I give a neat new booklet*
> *Polished up lately with dry pumice?*

In comparison with Goold this represents the diminutive *libellum* and the *ex* of *expolitum*, removes the ambiguity of 'pretty new', avoids translating the colourless *modo* as 'freshly', saves one syllable in the first line (to make up for the extra one in line 2), and provides an equivalent touch of alliteration there. One remembers the old saying 'Take care of the pence and the pounds will take care of themselves'; in translation 'the pence' are details like these—the minutiae.

But if the text of Catullus is here treated with the greatest respect, its metrical form is handled more freely. Catullus uses a variety of metres (for the details see Appendix B), and it is possible to reproduce them in English—possible but inadvisable, because only too often one has to resort to padding to fill up the requisite number of syllables. This can be seen at a glance by comparison of the original and the translation of Poem I. 1–2 above. Though the Latin has fewer words, it has more syllables than the English—nine words to fourteen, twenty-two syllables to eighteen.

Tennyson tried his hand at hendecasyllables and those attacking the 'chorus of indolent reviewers' are well known. Not so well known are his more truly Catullan lines in the same metre attacking J. H. Friswell and his collection of essays entitled *The Gentle Life*:

> *Gentle Life*—what a title! Here's a subject
> Calls aloud for a gentleman to handle!
> Who has handled it? he, the would-be poet,
> Friswell, Pisswell—a liar and a twaddler—
> Pisswell, Friswell—a clown beyond redemption,
> Brutal, personal, infinitely blackguard.

Stirring stuff, but difficult to do (and monotonous) in quantity. In fact experiment will show that a Catullan hendecasyllable can usually be rendered by nine English syllables, and Catullan iambics by English blank verse. As for the rarer metres, sapphics, asclepiads, etc., a similar attempt is made, if not to reproduce, at any rate to represent them.

A CHRONOLOGY

84 B.C. ? Birth of Catullus.

82   Sulla's victory over Marius' former supporters at the Colline Gate. Establishment of his dictatorship and restoration of senatorial authority. Savage proscriptions. Birth of Catullus' friend Calvus.

79   Sulla resigns his dictatorship and dies in 78.

77   Lepidus raises an army in northern Italy and marches on Rome. Defeated by Catulus and Pompey. Perperna with the remains of Lepidus' army joins the Marian governor Sertorius in Spain. Pompey sent against Sertorius.

74   Nicander IV of Bithynia dies, leaving his kingdom to Rome.

73   Spartacus, a Thracian gladiator, leads a slave revolt at Capua, recruits a powerful army and terrorizes Italy.

72   Sertorius murdered by Perperna. Pompey in control in Spain.

71   Spartacus defeated and killed by Crassus.

70   Pompey and Crassus consuls. Birth of Virgil.

67   Pompey's suppression of piracy in the Mediterranean.

66   Pompey given command against Mithridates of Pontus.

65   Birth of Horace.

63   Death of Mithridates. Pompey reorganizes Roman administration of the East. Cicero's consulship and suppression of the conspiracy of Catiline. Caesar elected Pontifex Maximus.

62   Metellus, Clodia's husband, governor of Cisalpine Gaul. Clodius, in drag, profanes the Mysteries of the Bona Dea (for women only) when held by Caesar's wife Pompeia.

60   The First Triumvirate, the political alliance of Pompey, Caesar, and Crassus. Metellus consul.

59   Death of Metellus. Caesar consul.

58   Clodius procures Cicero's banishment and tries to invalidate Caesar's legislation. Praetorship of Memmius, Lucretius' patron.

58–49 Caesar's campaigns in Gaul.

THE POEMS OF
CATULLUS
Text and Translation

I

Cui dono lepidum nouum libellum
arida modo pumice expolitum?
Corneli, tibi; namque tu solebas
meas esse aliquid putare nugas,
iam tum cum ausus es (unus Italorum)   5
omne aeuum tribus explicare chartis—
doctis, Iuppiter, et laboriosis!
quare habe tibi quidquid hoc libelli
qualecumque. quod, o Patrona Virgo,
plus uno maneat perenne saeclo.   10

II

Passer, deliciae meae puellae,
quicum ludere, quem in sinu tenere,
cui primum digitum dare appetenti
et acris solet incitare morsus
cum desiderio meo nitenti   5
karum nescioquid lubet iocari
et solaciolum sui doloris,
credo, ut tum grauis acquiescat ardor:
tecum ludere sicut ipsa possem
et tristis animi leuare curas!   10

II B

. . . . .

tam gratum est mihi quam ferunt puellae
pernici aureolum fuisse malum
quod zonam soluit diu ligatam.

III

Lugete, o Veneres Cupidinesque
et quantum est hominum uenustiorum:
passer mortuus est meae puellae,
passer, deliciae meae puellae,
quem plus illa oculis suis amabat.   5

I

Whom do I give a neat new booklet
Polished up lately with dry pumice?
You, Cornelius; for you always
Thought my trivia important,
Even when you dared (the one Italian)   5
Unfold the whole past in three papyri—
Learned, by Jupiter, and laborious!
So take this mere booklet for what it's worth,
Which may my Virgin Patroness
Keep fresh for more than one generation.   10

II

Sparrow, my girl's darling,
Whom she plays with, whom she cuddles,
Whom she likes to tempt with finger-
Tip and teases to nip harder
When my own bright-eyed desire   5
Fancies some endearing fun
And a small solace for her pain,
I suppose, so heavy passion then rests:
Would I could play with you as she does
And lighten the spirit's gloomy cares!   10

II B

. . . . .

It's welcome to me as they say
To fleet-foot girl was golden apple
That loosed the girdle tied too long.

III

Grieve, O Venuses and Loves
And all the lovelier people there are:
My girl's sparrow is dead,
Sparrow, my girl's darling,
Whom she loved more than her eyes.   5

nam mellitus erat suamque norat
ipsam tam bene quam puella matrem,
nec sese a gremio illius mouebat
sed circumsiliens modo huc modo illuc
ad solam dominam usque pipiabat. 10
qui nunc it per iter tenebricosum
illud unde negant redire quemquam.
at uobis male sit, malae tenebrae
Orci quae omnia bella deuoratis!
tam bellum mihi passerem abstulistis. 15
o factum male! o miselle passer!
tua nunc opera meae puellae
flendo turgiduli rubent ocelli.

IV

Phaselus ille quem uidetis, hospites,
ait fuisse nauium celerrimus
neque ullius natantis impetum trabis
nequisse praeterire, siue palmulis
opus foret uolare siue linteo. 5
et hoc negat minacis Hadriatici
negare litus insulasue Cycladas
Rhodumque nobilem horridamque Thracia
Propontida trucemue Ponticum sinum
ubi iste post phaselus antea fuit 10
comata silua; nam Cytorio in iugo
loquente saepe sibilum edidit coma.
Amastri Pontica et Cytore buxifer,
tibi haec fuisse et esse cognitissima
ait phaselus. ultima ex origine 15
tuo stetisse dicit in cacumine,
tuo imbuisse palmulas in aequore,
et inde tot per impotentia freta
erum tulisse, laeua siue dextera
uocaret aura, siue utrumque Iuppiter 20
simul secundus incidisset in pedem;
neque ulla uota litoralibus Deis
sibi esse facta cum ueniret a mari
nouissime hunc adusque limpidum lacum.

For honey-sweet he was and knew his
Mistress well as a girl her mother,
Nor would he ever leave her lap
But hopping around, this way, that way,
Kept cheeping to his lady alone.   10
And now he's off on the dark journey
From which they say no one returns.
Shame on you, shameful dark of Orcus,
For gobbling up all the pretty things!
You've robbed me of so pretty a sparrow.   15
O what a shame! O wretched sparrow!
Your fault it is that now my girl's
Eyelids are swollen red with crying.

IV

The sailing-boat you see there, visitors,
Claims to have been the speediest of ships
And not to have been incapable of passing
Any swimming timber if need be
By flying with either little palms or canvas.   5
And he denies the threatening Adriatic
Coast can deny this, the Cycladic islands,
Famous Rhodes, Propontis shivering
In Thracian gales or the grim Pontic gulf
Where he, the future boat, was first of all   10
A long-haired wood; for on Cytorus' top
His hair would often speak in a loud whisper.
Pontic Amastris and box-clad Cytorus,
To you these things were best known and still are,
The boat claims. In his distant origin   15
He says it was your summit that he stood on,
Your sea in which he dipped his little palms,
And from there through so many stormy straits
Carried his master, whether from left or right
The breeze was calling, or a following   20
Jupiter fell upon both feet at once.
Nor were there any vows to the shore Gods
Made for him as he voyaged finally
From the open sea right up to this clear lake.

sed haec prius fuere; nunc recondita   25
senet quiete seque dedicat tibi,
gemelle Castor et gemelle Castoris.

V

Vivamus, mea Lesbia, atque amemus
rumoresque senum seueriorum
omnes uniūs aestimemus assis.
soles occidere et redire possunt;
nobis, cum semel occidit breuis lux,   5
nox est perpetua una dormienda.
da mi basia mille, deinde centum,
dein mille altera, dein secunda centum,
deinde usque altera mille, deinde centum;
dein cum milia multa fecerimus   10
conturbabimus illa ne sciamus
aut ne quis malus inuidere possit
cum tantum sciat esse basiorum.

VI

Flaui, delicias tuas Catullo,
ni sint illepidae atque inelegantes,
uelles dicere nec tacere posses.
uerum nescioquid febriculosi
scorti diligis; hoc pudet fateri.   5
nam te non uiduas iacere noctes
nequiquam tacitum cubile clamat
sertis ac Syrio fragrans oliuo,
puluinusque peraeque et hic et ille
attritus, tremulique quassa lecti   10
argutatio inambulatioque.
nam nil ista ualet, nihil, tacere
cum non tam latera ecfututa pandas
ni tu quid facias ineptiarum.
quare quidquid habes boni malique   15
dic nobis. uolo te ac tuos amores
ad caelum lepido uocare uersu.

But that was in the past; now he grows old   25
In quiet retirement and devotes himself
To you, twin Castor, and you, Castor's twin.

V

We should live, my Lesbia, and love
And value all the talk of stricter
Old men at a single penny.
Suns can set and rise again;
For us, once our brief light has set,   5
There's one unending night for sleeping.
Give me a thousand kisses, then a hundred,
Then another thousand, then a second hundred,
Then still another thousand, then a hundred;
Then, when we've made many thousands,   10
We'll muddle them so as not to know
Or lest some villain overlook us
Knowing the total of our kisses.

VI

Were she not unsmart and unwitty,
Flavius, you'd want to tell Catullus
About your pet and couldn't keep quiet.
In fact you love some fever-ridden
Tart and you're ashamed to own it.   5
That you're not spending deprived nights
Silent in vain the bedroom shouts
Perfumed with flowers and Syrian oils,
The pillow equally this side and that
Dented, and the rickety bed's   10
Yackety perambulation.
It's no good keeping quiet about it.
You'd not present such fucked-out flanks
If you weren't up to something foolish.
So tell us what you've got, for good   15
Or ill. I wish to emparadise
You and your love in witty verse.

VII

Quaeris quot mihi basiationes
tuae, Lesbia, sint satis superque.
quam magnus numerus Libyssae harenae
lasarpiciferis iacet Cyrenis
oraclum Iouis inter aestuosi   5
et Batti ueteris sacrum sepulcrum,
aut quam sidera multa, cum tacet nox,
furtiuos hominum uident amores;
tam te basia multa basiare
uesano satis et super Catullo est,   10
quae nec pernumerare curiosi
possint nec mala fascinare lingua.

VIII

Miser Catulle, desinas ineptire
et quod uides perisse perditum ducas.
fulsere quondam candidi tibi soles
cum uentitabas quo puella ducebat
amata nobis quantum amabitur nulla.   5
ibi illa multa cum iocosa fiebant
quae tu uolebas nec puella nolebat,
fulsere uere candidi tibi soles.
nunc iam illa non uult; tu quoque, impotens, noli
nec quae fugit sectare nec miser uiue,   10
sed obstinata mente perfer, obdura.
uale, puella. iam Catullus obdurat
nec te requiret nec rogabit inuitam.
at tu dolebis cum rogaberis nulla.
scelesta, uae te, quae tibi manet uita?   15
quis nunc te adibit? cui uideberis bella?
quem nunc amabis? cuius esse diceris?
quem basiabis? cui labella mordebis?
at tu, Catulle, destinatus obdura.

VII

You ask how many of your mega-kisses
Would more than satisfy me, Lesbia.
Great as the sum of Libyssan sand lying
In silphiophorous Cyrene
From the oracle of torrid Jove   5
To old Battus' Holy Sepulchre,
Or many as the stars, when night is silent,
That watch the stolen loves of humans—
To kiss you just so many kisses
Would more than satisfy mad Catullus;   10
The inquisitive couldn't count them all
Nor evil tongue bring them bad luck.

VIII

Wretched Catullus, you should stop fooling
And what you know you've lost admit losing.
The sun shone brilliantly for you, time was,
When you kept following where a girl led you,
Loved by us as we shall love no one.   5
There when those many amusing things happened
Which you wanted nor did the girl not want
The sun shone brilliantly for you, truly.
Now she's stopped wanting, you must stop, weakling.
Don't chase what runs away nor live wretched   10
But with a mind made up be firm, stand fast.
Goodbye, girl. Catullus now stands fast,
Won't ask or look for you who're not willing.
But you'll be sorry when you're not asked for.
Alas, what life awaits you now, devil?   15
Who'll find you pretty now? What type touch you?
Whom will you love and whose be called henceforth?
Whom will you kiss? and you will bite whose lips?
But you, Catullus, mind made up, stand fast.

IX

Verani, omnibus e meis amicis
antestans mihi milibus trecentis,
uenistine domum ad tuos penates
fratresque unanimos anumque matrem?
uenisti. o mihi nuntii beati!   5
uisam te incolumem audiamque Hiberum
narrantem loca, facta, nationes,
ut mos est tuus, applicansque collum
iucundum os oculosque suauiabor.
o quantum est hominum beatiorum,   10
quid me laetius est beatiusue?

X

Varus me meus ad suos amores
uisum duxerat e foro otiosum,
scortillum, ut mihi tum repente uisum est,
non sane illepidum neque inuenustum.
huc ut uenimus, incidere nobis   5
sermones uarii, in quibus quid esset
iam Bithynia, quo modo se haberet,
et quonam mihi profuisset aere.
respondi id quod erat, nihil neque ipsis
nunc praetoribus esse nec cohorti   10
cur quisquam caput unctius referret,
praesertim quibus esset irrumator
praetor nec faceret pili cohortem.
'at certe tamen' inquiunt 'quod illic
natum dicitur esse comparasti—   15
ad lecticam homines.' ego ut puellae
unum me facerem beatiorem,
'non' inquam 'mihi tam fuit maligne
ut, prouincia quod mala incidisset,
non possem octo homines parare rectos.'   20
at mi nullus erat nec hic nequc illic
fractum qui ueteris pedem grabati
in collo sibi collocare posset.

IX

Veranius, of all my friends
The foremost by three hundred miles,
Have you come home to your household Gods
And like-minded brothers and old mother?
You have? O happy news for me!   5
I'll find you safe, hear you describing
Iberian places, exploits, tribes
In your own fashion. Embracing you
I'll kiss your merry face and eyes.
O of all the happier people   10
Who's happier or more glad than I?

X

Free in the Forum I was taken
By my Varus to meet his love,
A tartlet, as I thought at first,
By no means unwitty or unattractive.
Once arrived there we got talking   5
On various topics, including
Bithynia—how were things there now
And had it made me any brass?
I answered straight—there was nothing now
For praetors themselves or their staff,   10
Why anyone should come back flusher,
Especially when a shit's your praetor,
Who doesn't give a toss for staff.
'But surely' they said 'you collected
What's said to be the local product—   15
Bearers?' Whereat, to make the girl
Think me one of the luckier ones,
I said 'Things weren't so bad for me
Despite my drawing a bad province
That I could miss eight straight-backed men.'   20
In fact I'd no one, here or there,
To heave up on his head the broken
Leg of a second-hand camp-bed.

hic illa, ut decuit cinaediorem,
'quaeso,' inquit 'mihi, mi Catulle, paulum   25
istos commoda; nam uolo ad Serapim
deferri.' 'mane,' inquii puellae
'istud quod modo dixeram me habere,
fugit me ratio; meus sodalis—
Cinna est Gaius—is sibi parauit.   30
uerum utrum illius an mei quid ad me?
utor tam bene quam mihi pararim.
sed tu insulsa male et molesta uiuis
per quam non licet esse neglegentem.'

XI

Furi et Aureli, comites Catulli,
siue in extremos penetrabit Indos
litus ut longa resonante Eoa
tunditur unda,

siue in Hyrcanos Arabasue molles   5
seu Sacas sagittiferosue Parthos
siue quae septemgeminus colorat
aequora Nilus

siue trans altas gradietur Alpes
Caesaris uisens monimenta magni,   10
Gallicum Rhenum, horribiles uitro ulti-
mosque Britannos,

omnia haec, quaecumque feret uoluntas
Caelitum, temptare simul parati,
pauca nuntiate meae puellae   15
non bona dicta:

cum suis uiuat ualeatque moechis,
quos simul complexa tenet trecentos,
nullum amans uere, sed identidem omnium
ilia rumpens;   20

nec meum respectet, ut ante, amorem,
qui illius culpa cecidit uelut prati
ultimi flos, praetereunte postquam
tactus aratro est.

At this she said, like the bitch she was,
'Lend them to *me*, please, dear Catullus,   25
Just for a little. I need taking
To Sérapis.' 'Wait,' I replied
'What I said just now I had, I
Wasn't thinking. It's my messmate
Cinna—Gaius, you know—they're his.   30
But what's it matter whose they are?
I use them as if they were mine.
But you're damned tactless—a living nuisance
Who won't allow one to speak loosely.'

XI

Furius and Aurelius, Catullus' comrades,
Whether he'll push on to furthest India
Where the shore is pounded by far-resounding
Eoan rollers,

To Hyrcania or effeminate Arabia,   5
The Sacians or the arrow-bearing Parthians
Or those levels to which the seven-double
Nilus gives colour,

Or make his way across the towering Alps
To visit the memorials of great Caesar,   10
The Gallic Rhine, those horrible woad-painted
And world's-end Britons—

All this, whatever the will of Heaven above
May bring, ready as you are to brave together,
Simply deliver to my girl a brief dis-   15
courteous message:

Farewell and long life with her adulterers,
Three hundred together, whom hugging she holds,
Loving none truly but again and again
Rupturing all's groins;   20

And let her not as before expect my love,
Which by her fault has fallen like a flower
On the meadow's margin after a passing
Ploughshare has touched it.

XII

Marrucine Asini, manu sinistra
non belle uteris; in ioco atque uino
tollis lintea neglegentiorum.
hoc salsum esse putas? fugit te, inepte.
quamuis sordida res et inuenusta est.   5
non credis mihi? crede Pollioni
fratri, qui tua furta uel talento
mutari uelit. est cnim leporum
differtus puer ac facetiarum.
quare aut hendecasyllabos trecentos   10
expecta aut mihi linteum remitte,
quod me non mouet aestimatione,
uerum est mnemosynum mei sodalis.
nam sudaria Saetaba ex Hiberis
miserunt mihi muneri Fabullus   15
et Veranius. haec amem necesse est
ut Veraniolum meum et Fabullum.

XIII

Cenabis bene, mi Fabulle, apud me
paucis, si tibi Di fauent, diebus,
si tecum attuleris bonam atque magnam
cenam non sine candida puella
et uino et sale et omnibus cachinnis.   5
haec si, inquam, attuleris, uenuste noster,
cenabis bene; nam tui Catulli
plenus sacculus est aranearum.
sed contra accipies meros amores
seu quid suauius elegantiusue est;   10
nam unguentum dabo quod meae puellae
donarunt Veneres Cupidinesque,
quod tu cum olfacies, deos rogabis
totum ut te faciant, Fabulle, nasum.

XII

Márrucine Asínius, you misuse
Your left hand; while we joke and drink
You lift the napkins of the careless.
You think it clever? You're wrong, you fool.
It's a downright dirty and vulgar trick.   5
You don't believe me? Believe Pollio
Your brother, who would gladly give
A talent to undo your thefts.
For he's a boy full of wit and charm.
Return my napkin, then, or expect   10
Three hundred hendecasyllables.
I'm not concerned about its value,
But it's a memento of my comrade.
For Veranius and Fabullus sent me
Saetaban napkins as a gift from Spain.   15
So I must love them like my dear
Fabullus and Verániolus.

XIII

You'll dine well, my Fabullus, at mine
One day soon if the Gods are kind to you,
If you will bring with you a dinner
Good and large plus a pretty girl
And wine and salt and all the laughs.   5
It, I repeat, you bring these with you,
Our charmer, you'll dine well; for your
Catullus' purse is full of cobwebs.
But in return you'll get love neat
Or something still more choice and fragrant;   10
For I'll provide the perfume given
My girl by Venuses and Cupids
And when you smell it you'll ask the Gods,
Fabullus, to make you one large nose.

XIV

Ni te plus oculis meis amarem,
iucundissime Calue, munere isto
odissem te odio Vatiniano.
nam quid feci ego quidue sum locutus
cur me tot male perderes poetis?   5
isti Di mala multa dent clienti
qui tantum tibi misit impiorum.
quod si, ut suspicor, hoc nouum ac repertum
munus dat tibi Sulla litterator,
non est mi male sed bene ac beate   10
quod non dispereunt tui labores.
di magni, horribilem et sacrum libellum!
quem tu scilicet ad tuum Catullum
misti continuo ut die periret
Saturnalibus, optimo dierum!   15
non, non hoc tibi, salse, sic abibit.
nam si luxerit, ad librariorum
curram scrinia; Caesios, Aquinos,
Suffenum, omnia colligam uenena,
ac te his suppliciis remunerabor.   20
uos hinc interea ualete abite
illuc unde malum pedem attulistis,
saecli incommoda, pessimi poetae.

XIV B

Si qui forte mearum ineptiarum
lectores eritis manusque uestras
non horrebitis admouere nobis
· · · · ·

XV

Commendo tibi me ac meos amores,
Aureli. ueniam peto pudentem
ut, si quicquam animo tuo cupisti
quod castum expeteres et integellum,
conserues puerum mihi pudice,   5

XIV

Did I not love you more than my eyes,
Calvus you joker, then for that gift
I'd hate you with Vatinian hatred.
What have I done to you or said
That you should pip me with all these poets?   5
May Gods bring curses on the client
Who sent you such profanities.
And if, as I suspect, this choice new
Gift to you is from schoolmaster Sulla,
Then I'm not sorry but delighted   10
That your hard work has not been wasted.
Great Gods, a damned awful little book
For you to send to your Catullus
To kill him outright on that day
Of all days best—the Saturnalia.   15
No, you won't get away with it,
Clever dick. When it's dawn I'll run
To the bookstalls, pick up all the poison—
Suffenus, Caesius and Aquinus—
And pay you back with pains like them.   20
Meanwhile goodbye, be off with you,
Back where you brought your faulty feet from,
Curse of our time, appalling poets!

XIV B

If maybe any of you there are
Who read my follies and you don't
Shudder to lay your hands on us

. . . . .

XV

Recommending to you my love and me,
Aurelius, I ask a modest favour—
That if in your heart you've ever longed
To seek out something pure and unspoiled,
You'll guard the boy for me modestly,   5

non dico a populo—nihil ueremur
istos qui in platea modo huc modo illuc
in re praetereunt sua occupati—
uerum a te metuo tuoque pene
infesto pueris bonis malisque.   10
quem tu qua lubet, ut lubet, moueto
quantum uis ubi erit foris paratum;
hunc unum excipio, ut puto, pudenter.
quod si te mala mens furorque uecors
in tantam impulerit, sceleste, culpam   15
ut nostrum insidiis caput lacessas,
a, tum te miserum malique fati,
quem attractis pedibus patente porta
percurrent raphanique mugilesque!

XVI

Pedicabo ego uos et irrumabo,
Aureli pathice et cinaede Furi,
qui me ex uersiculis meis putastis,
quod sunt molliculi, parum pudicum.
nam castum esse decet pium poetam   5
ipsum, uersiculos nihil necesse est;
qui tum denique habent salem ac leporem
si sunt molliculi ac parum pudici
et quod pruriat incitare possunt,
non dico pueris sed his pilosis   10
qui duros nequeunt mouere lumbos.
uos, quod milia multa basiorum
legistis, male me marem putatis?
pedicabo ego uos et irrumabo.

XVII

O Colonia quae cupis

                    ponte ludere longo
et salire paratum habes

                  sed uereris inepta
crura ponticuli axulis

                  stantis in rediuiuis

Not from the public—I'm not afraid
Of those going to and fro about
The square intent on their own business—
It's you I'm scared of and your penis,
That menace to good boys and bad.   10
Wield it anywhere and -how
Ad lib, given the chance, outside,
With this one, I think, modest exception.
But should ill will or mindless madness
Drive you, villain, to the crime   15
Of treachery against my person,
Ah then you'll rue your wretched fate
With feet trussed up and backdoor open,
Run through with radishes and mullet.

XVI

I'll bugger you and stuff your gobs,
Aurelius Kink and Pootter Furius,
For thinking me, because my verses
Are rather sissy, not quite decent.
For the true poet should be chaste   5
Himself, his verses need not be.
Indeed they've salt and charm then only
When rather sissy and not quite decent
And when they can excite an itch
I don't say in boys but in those hairy   10
Victims of lumbar sclerosis.
Because you've read of my x thousand
Kisses you doubt my virility?
I'll bugger you and stuff your gobs.

XVII

O Colonia, so keen to
                    celebrate on your long bridge
And all set for dancing there but
                    frightened of the rickety
Legs of the poor old bridge propped up
                    on resurrected timbers

ne supinus eat cauaque
in palude recumbat;
sic tibi bonus ex tua
pons libidine fiat   5
in quo uel Salisubsali
sacra suscipiantur,
munus hoc mihi maximi
da, Colonia, risus:
quendam municipem meum
de tuo uolo ponte
ire praecipitem in lutum
per caputque pedesque,
uerum totius ut lacus
putidaeque paludis   10
liuidissima maximeque
est profunda uorago.
insulsissimus est homo
nec sapit pueri instar
bimuli tremula patris
dormientis in ulna.
cui cum sit uiridissimo
nupta flore puella,
et puella tenellulo
delicatior haedo,   15
adseruanda nigerrimis
diligentius uuis,
ludere hanc sinit ut lubet
nec pili facit uni
nec se subleuat ex sua
parte sed uelut alnus
in fossa Liguri iacet
suppernata securi,
tantundem omnia sentiens
quam si nulla sit usquam.   20
talis iste meus stupor
nil uidet, nihil audit;
ipse qui sit, utrum sit an
non sit, id quoque nescit.
nunc eum uolo de tuo
ponte mittere pronum,

In case it falls flat on its back
          and settles in the deep bog,
May a good bridge be built for you
          exactly to your liking   5
Where even Salisubsalus
          in safety can be worshipped,
Provided that you play for me
          this best of jokes, Colonia,
On a fellow townsman of mine:
          I'd like him to be thrown down
Slap into the mud from your
          bridge head over heels
Precisely where in all the lake
          and evil-smelling marsh   10
There is the deepest quagmire and
          most livid-looking mud.
The creature is a perfect fool
          with less sense than a child,
A two-year-old who's fast asleep
          rocked in his father's arms.
For though he's married to a girl
          who's in her greenest flower,
A girl indeed more frivolous
          than any tender kidling,   15
Who needs more careful watching than
          the very blackest grapes,
He lets her fool around at will
          and doesn't turn a hair
And doesn't rise up for his part
          but lies there like an alder
That's lying in a ditch hamstrung
          by a Ligurian hatchet,
As much aware of everything
          as though she didn't exist.   20
Yes, this perfect dolt of mine
          sees nothing and hears nothing,
Not knowing who he really is
          or if he is at all.
Now, I'd like to throw him down
          headlong from your bridge

si pote stolidum repente
                excitare ueternum
et supinum animum in graui
                derelinquere caeno,   25
ferream ut soleam tenaci
                in uoragine mula.

XXI

Aureli, pater esuritionum,
non harum modo sed quot aut fuerunt
antehac aut aliis erunt in annis,
pedicare cupis mcos amores,
nec clam. nam simul es, iocaris una,   5
haerens ad latus omnia experiris.
frustra, nam insidias mihi instruentem
tangam te prior irrumatione.
atque id si faceres satur, tacerem;
nunc ipsum id doleo quod esurire   10
a temet puer et sitire discet.
quare desine dum licet pudico,
ne finem facias sed irrumatus.

XXII

Suffenus iste, Vare, quem probe nosti
homo est uenustus et dicax et urbanus,
idemque longe plurimos facit uersus.
puto esse ego illi milia aut decem aut plura
perscripta, nec sicut fit in palimpsesto   5
relata; chartae regiae noui libri,
noui umbilici, lora rubra, membranae,
derecta plumbo et pumice omnia aequata.
haec cum legas tu, bellus ille et urbanus
Suffenus unus caprimulgus aut fossor   10
rursus uidetur; tantum abhorret ac mutat.
hoc quid putemus esse? qui modo scurra
aut siquid hac re tritius uidebatur,
idem infaceto est infacetior rurc
simul poemata attigit, neque idem umquam   15
aeque est beatus ac poema cum scribit;

To see if he can suddenly
                    shake off his stupid sloth
And leave behind his spineless
                    spirit in the mire   25
As a mule leaves her iron
                    shoe in the clinging clay.

XXI

Aurelius, father of the hungers,
Not just of these but of all that were
Ere this or will be in other years,
You long to bugger my love, and not
In secret. You're with him, sharing jokes,   5
Close at his side, trying everything.
It's no good. If you plot against me
I'll get in first and stuff your gob.
I'd keep quiet if you did it well fed;
But it annoys me that the boy   10
Will learn from you to hunger and thirst.
So stop it while you decently may,
In case you make your end—gob-stuffed.

XXII

Dear Varus, your not improper intimate Suffenus
Is a charming person, witty and urbane;
Besides, his verse production is enormous—
Ten thousand lines, I calculate, or more.
He's written out, and not on palimpsest   5
Like most folk—no, new rolls of royal papyrus,
New bosses, scarlet thongs and parchment covers,
The whole lead-ruled and levelled off with pumice.
But when you read them, that nice urbane man
Suffenus now seems a mere clodhopper   10
Or boor, he's so unlike himself, so changed.
How to explain it? The man who just now seemed
A city wit, or something smoother still,
Even so is clumsier than the clumsy country
Whenever he tries poetry—and yet   15
He's never as happy as when poetizing.

tam gaudet in se tamque se ipse miratur.
nimirum idem omnes fallimur, neque est quisquam
quem non in aliqua re uidere Suffenum
possis. suus cuique attributus est error,   20
sed non uidemus manticae quod in tergo est.

XXIII

Furi, cui neque seruus est neque arca
nec cimex neque araneus neque ignis,
uerum est pater et nouerca quorum
dentes uel silicem comesse possunt,
est pulcrc tibi cum tuo parente   5
et cum coniuge lignea parentis.
nec mirum: bene nam ualetis omnes,
pulcre concoquitis, nihil timetis,
non incendia, non graues ruinas,
non facta impia, non dolos ueneni,   10
non casus alios periculorum.
atqui corpora sicciora cornu
aut siquid magis aridum est habetis
sole et frigore et esuritione.
quare non tibi sit bene ac beate?   15
a te sudor abest, abest saliua
mucusque et mala pituita nasi.
hanc ad munditiem adde mundiorem,
quod culus tibi purior salillo est
nec toto decies cacas in anno,   20
atque id durius est faba et lupillis,
quod tu si manibus teras fricesque,
non umquam digitum inquinare possis.
haec tu commoda tam beata, Furi,
noli spernere nec putare parui,   25
et sestertia quae soles precari
centum desine, nam sat es beatus.

XXIV

O qui flosculus es Iuuentiorum,
non horum modo sed quot aut fuerunt

He's so pleased with himself, thinks he's so marvellous.
We all, I fancy, have that fault. There's no one
Who's not, you'll find, *suffenous* in some way.
Each person's stuck with his peculiar failing,   20
But we can't see the sack we're carrying.

XXIII

Furius, you've no slave or cash-box,
You've no spider, bug, or fire,
But a father and stepmother
Whose teeth can even chew through flint.
A splendid time you have with father   5
And with father's wooden wife.
No wonder, for you're all in good health,
Digest splendidly, fear nothing,
Not fires or houses falling down,
Crimes of violence, poison plots,   10
Or other dangerous circumstance.
Besides you've bodies drier than horn,
Or whatever's even more dehydrated,
From sun and cold and hungriness.
Why shouldn't you be well and happy?   15
You never sweat, you've no saliva,
No mucus, no nasal catarrh.
That's hygiene. This is more hygienic:
An arsehole clean as a saltcellar;
You shit less than ten times a year   20
And then it's hard as beans and lupins
And if you rubbed it in your hands
You'd never dirty a single finger.
These are rich blessings, Furius;
Don't undervalue or despise them   25
And do stop begging for that hundred
Thousand—you're rich enough already.

XXIV

O flower of the Juventii,
Not just of these but of all that were

aut posthac aliis erunt in annis,
mallem diuitias Midae dedisses
isti cui neque seruus est neque arca 5
quam sic te sineres ab illo amari.
'qui? non est homo bellus?' inquies. est,
sed bello huic neque seruus est neque arca.
hoc tu quam lubet abice eleuaque,
nec seruum tamen ille habet neque arcam. 10

XXV

Cinaede Thalle, mollior
  cuniculi capillo
uel anseris medullula
  uel imula oricilla
uel pene languido senis
  situque araneoso,
idemque, Thalle, turbida
  rapacior procella
cum Diua miluorum aues
  ostendit oscitantes, 5
remitte pallium mihi
  meum quod inuolasti
sudariumque Saetabum
  catagraphosque Thynos,
inepte, quae palam soles
  habere tamquam auita.
quae nunc tuis ab unguibus
  reglutina et remitte,
ne laneum latusculum
  manusque mollicellas 10
inusta turpiter tibi
  conscribilent flagella,
et insolenter aestues,
  uelut minuta magno
deprensa nauis in mari,
  uesaniente uento.

Or will be later in other years,
I'd rather you gave Midas' riches
To that man without slave or cash-box   5
Than let him love you as you do.
'He's a nice man' you'll say. Yes, but
His niceness has no slave or cash-box.
Demur if you must, make light of it,
Still he has neither slave nor cash-box.   10

XXV

Fairy Thallus, softer than
                    a little furry bunny
Or a goosey's marrow or
                    a teeny-weeny ear-lobe
Or an old man's drooping penis
                    or a spider's dust trap,
But also, Thallus, more rapacious
                    than the wildest whirlwind
Whenever the Goddess of hawks
                    gives notice birds are napping,   5
Send back to me that cloak of mine
                    you've swooped upon and stolen
And the Spanish napkin too
                    and those Bithynian face-towels
Which, tasteless idiot, you keep
                    exhibiting as heirlooms.
Unglue them pronto from your crooked
                    talons and return them,
For fear your flabby little flanks
                    and namby-pamby handies   10
Are branded in an ugly way
                    and scribbled on with lashes,
And there you are—on heat and tossed
                    so differently, just like
A baby boat in a big sea
                    caught by a roaring storm-wind.

XXVI

Furi, uillula uestra non ad Austri
flatus opposita est neque ad Fauoni
nec saeui Boreae aut Apheliotae,
uerum ad milia quindecim et ducentos.
o uentum horribilem atque pestilentem!   5

XXVII

Minister uetuli puer Falerni,
inger mi calices amariores
ut lex Postumiae iubet magistrae
ebrioso acino ebriosioris.
at uos quo lubet hinc abite, lymphae,   5
uini pernicies, et ad seueros
migrate. hic merus est Thyonianus.

XXVIII

Pisonis comites, cohors inanis
aptis sarcinulis et expeditis,
Verani optime tuque mi Fabulle,
quid rerum geritis? satisne cum isto
uappa frigoraque et famem tulistis?   5
ecquidnam in tabulis patet lucelli
expensum ut mihi qui meum secutus
praetorem refero datum lucello?
o Memmi, bene me ac diu supinum
tota ista trabe lentus irrumasti.   10
sed quantum uideo pari fuistis
casu, nam nihilo minore uerpa
farti estis. pete nobiles amicos!
at uobis mala multa Di Deaeque
dent, opprobria Romuli Remique.   15

XXIX

Quis hoc potest uidere, quis potest pati
nisi impudicus et uorax et aleo,

XXVI

Furius, your little countryhouse faces
Not draughts of Auster or Favonius
Or savage Boreas or Apheliotes
But fifteen thousand tenscore sesterces,
An overdraft that's not good for your health.   5

XXVII

Boy server of old Falernian,
Pour me out more pungent cups
As toastmistress Postumia rules,
Who's drunker than the drunken grape.
Pure water, find your level elsewhere.   5
You ruin wine. Shift to the sober.
Here is unmixed Thyonian.

XXVIII

Piso's lieutenants, needy staff
With baggage packed and portable,
Best Veranius and my Fabullus,
How are you doing? With that creep
You've had your fill of cold and hunger?   5
Do your accounts show any profit,
As mine do costs? In service with
My praetor I enter debt as profit.
O Memmius, you've laid me, good and long
Stuffed me with all that yard of yours.   10
You two, as far as I can see,
Have fared the same—stuffed by no less
A prick. Find noble friends, they say!
Heaven bring the plagues upon that pair
Of slurs on Romulus and Remus!   15

XXIX

Who can watch this, who suffer it, unless
He's shameless and a glutton and a gambler—

Mamurram habere quod Comata Gallia
habebat uncti et ultima Britannia?
cinaede Romule, haec uidebis et feres?   5
et ille nunc superbus et superfluens
perambulabit omnium cubilia
ut albulus columbus aut Adoneus?
cinaede Romule, haec uidebis et feres?
es impudicus et uorax et aleo.   10
eone nomine, imperator unice,
fuisti in ultima occidentis insula
ut ista uestra diffututa mentula
ducenties comesset aut trecenties?
quid est alid sinistra liberalitas?   15
parum expatrauit an parum helluatus est?
paterna prima lancinata sunt bona,
secunda praeda Pontica, inde tertia
Hibera, quam scit amnis aurifer Tagus.
et huicne Gallia et metet Britannia?   20
quid hunc, malum, fouetis? aut quid hic potest
nisi uncta deuorare patrimonia?
eone nomine, Vrbis o piissimi,
socer generque, perdidistis omnia?

XXX

Alfene immemor atque unanimis false
        sodalibus,
iam te nil miseret, dure, tui dulcis
        amiculi?
iam me prodere, iam non dubitas fallere,
        perfide?
nec facta impia fallacum hominum caelicolis
        placent,
quod tu neglegis ac me miserum deseris in malis.   5
eheu, quid faciant, dic, homines cuiue habeant fidem?
certe tute iubebas animam tradere, inique, me
inducens in amorem, quasi tuta omnia mi forent.
idem nunc retrahis te ac tua dicta omnia
        factaque

Mamurra having all the fat that long-haired
Gaul and remotest Britain used to have?
Poof Romulus, you'll watch this and allow it?   5
That supercilious and superfluous figure
Prancing about in everybody's bedroom
Like a white lovey-dovey or Adoneus?
Poof Romulus, you'll watch this and allow it?
You're shameless and a glutton and a gambler.   10
Was it for this, O Generalissimo,
You've been in that far island of the west,
So that your pal, that multifucking tool,
Could eat his way through twenty or thirty million?
Cack-handed generosity—that's what!   15
Surely he's leched and gormandized enough?
In the first place he blued his patrimony,
Second, the Pontic loot, and third the Spanish,
As Tagus, that gold-bearing river, knows.
And for this man shall Gaul and Britain reap?   20
Why patronize *him*, damn it! What's he good for
Except to gobble up fat private fortunes?
Was it for this, you most devoted Romans,
Father- and son-in-law, you've ruined all?

XXX

Alfenus, forgetful and treacherous to your close
        companions,
Does your hard heart now feel no pity for your
        'sweet friend'?
Traitor, are you not loth after all to betray and deceive
        me?
The Dwellers in Heaven abhor deceitful men's impious
        deeds.
This you disdain and desert wretched me in my troubles.   5
Tell me, alas, what can folk do or whom can they trust?
Cheat, it was certainly you bade me surrender my soul,
Luring me into love, as if all would be safe for me.
Now you back out and allow the winds and the airy
        clouds

uentos irrita ferre ac nebulas aereas
    sinis.   10
si tu oblitus es, at Di meminerunt, meminit
    Fides,
quae te ut paeniteat postmodo facti faciet
    tui.

XXXI

Paene insularum, Sirmio, insularumque
ocelle, quascumque in liquentibus stagnis
marique uasto fert uterque Neptunus,
quam te libenter quamque laetus inuiso,
uix mi ipse credens Thyniam atque Bithynos   5
liquisse campos et uidere te in tuto.
o quid solutis est beatius curis,
cum mens onus reponit ac peregrino
labore fessi uenimus Larem ad nostrum
desideratoque acquiescimus lecto?   10
hoc est quod unum est pro laboribus tantis.
salue, o uenusta Sirmio, atque ero gaude
gaudente, uosque, o Lydiae lacus undae,
ridete quidquid est domi cachinnorum.

XXXII

Amabo, mea dulcis Ipsitilla,
meae deliciae, mei lepores,
iube ad te ueniam meridiatum,
et si iusseris, illud adiuuato,
nequis liminis obseret tabellam   5
neu tibi lubeat foras abire,
sed domi maneas paresque nobis
nouem continuas fututiones.
uerum siquid ages, statim iubeto;
nam pransus iaceo et satur supinus   10
pertundo tunicamque palliumque.

To carry away unfulfilled all of your words and
    deeds.   10
You may forget, but the Gods remember, Good Faith
    remembers,
And she will later make sure that you wish what you did
    were undone.

XXXI

Of almost islands, Sirmio, and islands
The jewel—of all that either Neptune bears
In clear lake-water or desolate ocean,
How pleased, how happy I am to see you again,
Hardly convinced that I have left Thynia   5
And the Bithynian plains and found you safe.
O what more blissful than to have no worries,
When mind lays down the load, and tired of foreign
Service we have come to our own Lar
And rest content upon the longed-for bed!   10
This on its own makes up for all the hardship.
Greetings, delightful Sirmio. Enjoy your
Master's joy, and you, the lake's Lydian waves,
Laugh with all the mirth you have at home.

XXXII

Please, my love, sweet Ipsitilla,
My darling, my own clever girl,
Command my presence at siesta
And if you do, help by ensuring
That no one bolts your outer door   5
And that you don't go out on impulse
But stay home and prepare for us
Nine uninterrupted fuctions.
In fact if you're willing command me now.
I lie back after a large lunch   10
Boring holes in tunic and cloak.

XXXIII

O furum optime balneariorum,
Vibenni pater, et cinaede fili,
(nam dextra pater inquinatiore,
culo filius est uoraciore)
cur non exilium malasque in oras   5
itis, quandoquidem patris rapinae
notae sunt populo, et natis pilosas,
fili, non potes asse uenditare?

XXXIV

Dianae sumus in fide,
puellae et pueri integri.
Dianam, pueri integri
puellaeque, canamus.

o Latonia, maximi   5
magna progenies Iouis,
quam mater prope Deliam
deposiuit oliuam,

montium domina ut fores
siluarumque uirentium   10
saltuumque reconditorum
amniumque sonantum:

tu Lucina dolentibus
Iuno dicta puerperis,
tu potens Triuia et notho es   15
dicta lumine Luna.

tu cursu, Dea, menstruo
metiens iter annuum,
rustica agricolae bonis
tecta frugibus exples.   20

sis quocumque tibi placet
sancta nomine, Romulique
antique ut solita es bona
sospites ope gentem.

XXXIII

O best of thieves in the public baths,
Father Vibennius, and faggot son,
(Father's right hand is filthier,
Son's arsehole more acquisitive)
Be off to exile and perdition!   5
Why not, when father's larcenies
Are known to all and son can't sell
His hairy buttocks for one penny?

XXXIV

In Diana's trust are we,
Girls and boys unblemished.
Of Diana, unblemished boys
And girls, let us sing.

O Latona's daughter, great   5
Progeny of greatest Jove,
Whom thy mother bore beside
The Delian olive,

To be mistress of mountains
And the greening forests   10
And unfrequented passes
And strident streams:

Thou art called Lucina Juno
By women in labour pains,
Called powerful Three-Ways and Moon   15
Of borrowed light.

Goddess, by Thy monthly course
Measuring the year's journey
Thou fillest up with good fruits
The farmer's barns.   20

Hallowed be Thou by the name
Of Thy pleasure, and protect
As in days of old from ill
Romulus' race.

XXXV

Poetae tenero, meo sodali,
uelim Caecilio, papyre, dicas
Veronam ueniat, Noui relinquens
Comi moenia Lariumque litus.
nam quasdam uolo cogitationes   5
amici accipiat sui meique.
quare, si sapiet, uiam uorabit,
quamuis candida milies puella
euntem reuocat manusque collo
ambas iniciens roget morari.   10
quae nunc, si mihi uera nuntiantur,
illum deperit impotente amore.
nam quo tempore legit incohatam
Dindymi Dominam, ex eo misellae
ignes interiorem edunt medullam.   15
ignosco tibi, Sapphica puella
Musa doctior; est enim uenuste
Magna Caecilio incohata Mater.

XXXVI

Annales Volusi, cacata charta,
uotum soluite pro mea puella.
nam sanctae Veneri Cupidinique
uouit, si sibi restitutus essem
desissemque truces uibrare iambos,   5
electissima pessimi poetac
scripta tardipedi Deo daturam
infelicibus ustulanda lignis.
et hoc pessima se puella uidit
iocose lepide uouere Diuis.   10
nunc, o caeruleo creata ponto,
quae sanctum Idalium Vriosque apertos
quaeque Ancona Cnidumque harundinosam
colis quaeque Amathunta quaeque Golgos
quaeque Dyrrachium, Hadriae tabernam,   15
acceptum face redditumque uotum,
si non illepidum neque inuenustum est.

XXXV

I'd like you, papyrus, to tell my comrade
Caecilius, the tender poet,
To come to Verona, leaving Novum
Comum's walls and the Larian shore.
I want him to consider certain   5
Thoughts of a friend of his and mine.
So if he's wise he'll eat up the road,
Though a pretty girl should call him back
A thousand times and laying both
Hands on his neck should beg him stay.   10
There's one now, if I'm rightly informed,
Dying of desperate love for him.
For ever since the day she read
His unfinished *Lady of Dindymus*
Fires have been eating the poor thing's marrow.   15
And I don't blame you, girl more learned
Than Sappho's Muse. Caecilius' *Great
Mother* is charmingly unfinished.

XXXVI

Volusius' *Annals*, paper crap,
Redeem a vow in my girl's name.
She vowed to Cupid and St Venus
That if I were restored to her
And ceased to hurl savage iambics   5
She'd offer the worst poet's choicest
Work to the Hobble-footed God
For frizzling on funereal firewood.
The worst of girls intended this
Vow to the Gods as a witty joke.   10
So, Daughter of the dark-blue Deep,
Who hauntest holy Idalium,
Bleak Urii, Ancona, reedy
Cnidus, Amathus and Golgi
And Hadria's tavern, Dyrrachium,   15
Record the vow as duly paid,
If it's not lacking wit and charm.

at uos interea uenite in ignem,
pleni ruris et inficetiarum
Annales Volusi, cacata charta.   20

XXXVII

Salax taberna uosque contubernales,
a Pilleatis nona Fratribus pila,
solis putatis esse mentulas uobis,
solis licere quidquid est puellarum
confutuere et putere ceteros hircos?   5
an continenter quod sedetis insulsi
centum an ducenti, non putatis ausurum
me una ducentos irrumare sessores?
atqui putate: namque totius uobis
frontem tabernae sopionibus scribam.   10
puella nam mi, quae meo sinu fugit,
amata tantum quantum amabitur nulla,
pro qua mihi sunt magna bella pugnata,
consedit istic. hanc boni beatique
omnes amatis, et quidem (quod indignum est)   15
omnes pusilli et semitarii moechi;
tu praeter omnes, une de capillatis,
cuniculosae Celtiberiae fili,
Egnati, opaca quem bonum facit barba
et dens Hibera defricatus urina.   20

XXXVIII

Male est, Cornifici, tuo Catullo,
male est, me Hercule, et laboriose,
et magis magis in dies et horas.
quem tu, quod minimum facillimumque est,
qua solatus es allocutione?   5
irascor tibi. sic meos amores?
paulum quid lubet allocutionis
maestius lacrimis Simonideis.

But you meanwhile shall fuel the flames,
You load of rural crudities,
Volusius' *Annals*, paper crap.   20

XXXVII

Randy Inn and all you 'Inn-attendants',
Ninth pillar from the Brothers with Felt Hats,
D'you reckon you're the only ones with tools,
The only ones allowed to fuck the girls
And that the rest of us are stinking goats?   5
Or, since you clots are sitting in a queue
One or two hundred strong, d'you think I wouldn't
Dare stuff two hundred sitting tenants at once?
Well, think again. For I shall scrawl the Inn's
Whole frontage for you with phallic graffiti—   10
Because a girl who ran from my embrace,
Loved by me as no other will be loved,
For whom a great war has been fought by me,
Has settled here. With her the good and great
Are all in love and what's more (shame upon her!)   15
All the shoddy backstreet adulterers.
You above all, ace of the longhaired mob,
A son of rabbit-ridden Celtiberia,
Egnatius, whom a shady beard upgrades
And teeth rubbed down with Iberian urine.   20

XXXVIII

It's bad, Cornificius, with your Catullus,
It's bad, by Hercules, hard labour,
And more and more so each day and hour.
But have you (what's least and easiest)
Offered him any consolation?   5
I'm angry with you. So much for my love?
Please, any scrap of consolation
Sadder than tears of Simonides.

XXXIX

Egnatius, quod candidos habet dentes,
renidet usquequaque. si ad rei uentum est
subsellium, cum orator excitat fletum,
renidet ille. si ad pii rogum fili
lugetur, orba cum flet unicum mater,   5
renidet ille. quidquid est, ubicumque est,
quodcumque agit, renidet. hunc habet morbum,
neque elegantem, ut arbitror, ncquc urbanum.
quare monendum est te mihi, bone Egnati.
si urbanus esses aut Sabinus aut Tiburs   10
aut parcus Umber aut obesus Etruscus
aut Lanuuinus ater atque dentatus
aut Transpadanus, ut meos quoque attingam,
aut quilubet qui puriter lauit dentes,
tamen renidere usquequaquc te nollem,   15
nam risu inepto res ineptior nulla est.
nunc Celtiber es: Celtiberia in terra,
quod quisque minxit, hoc sibi solet mane
dentem atque russam defricare gingiuam;
ut quo iste uester expolitior dens est,   20
hoc te amplius bibisse praedicet loti.

XL

Quaenam te mala mens, miselle Rauide,
agit praecipitem in meos iambos?
quis Deus tibi non bene aduocatus
uecordem parat excitare rixam?
an ut peruenias in ora uulgi?   5
quid uis? qualubet esse notus optas?
eris, quandoquidem meos amores
cum longa uoluisti amare poena.

XLI

Amcana, puclla defututa,
tota milia me decem poposcit,
ista turpiculo puella naso,

XXXIX

Because Egnatius has white shiny teeth
He's always grinning. In court on the defendant's
Side while Counsel's turning on the tears
He grins. At a devoted son's cremation
While stricken mother mourns her only boy   5
He grins. Whatever's happening, wherever,
However employed, he grins. He has this tic,
Not, in my view, attractive or polite.
So here's a thought for you, my good Egnatius.
If you were Roman, Sabine or Tiburtine   10
Or stingy Umbrian or obese Etruscan
Or dark Lanuvian with rabbit teeth
Or (not forgetting my own folk) Transpadane
Or anyone who cleans his teeth with water
I'd still not like you to be always grinning.   15
Nothing's more fatuous than a fatuous smile.
But you're Celtiberian and in Celtiberia
Everyone uses his own pee each morning
For rubbing down his teeth and his red gums.
So the more highly polished your teeth are   20
The more the piddle you are proved to have drunk.

XL

What bad thinking, wretched Ravidus,
Drives you straight into my iambics?
What God unluckily invoked
Involves you in a stupid feud?
You want to live on vulgar lips,   5
Notorious at any cost?
You shall be, as you've chosen to love
My love and pay the long-term price.

XLI

Ameana, the female fuck-up,
Has asked me for a cool ten thousand,
That girl with the unattractive nose,

decoctoris amica Formiani.
propinqui quibus est puella curae,   5
amicos medicosque conuocate.
non est sana puella, nec rogare
qualis sit solet aes imaginosum.

XLII

Adeste, Hendecasyllabi quot estis
omnes, undique quotquot estis omnes.
iocum me putat esse moecha turpis
et negat mihi nostra reddituram
pugillaria, si pati potestis.   5
persequamur eam et reflagitemus.
quae sit quaeritis? illa quam uidetis
turpe incedere, mimice ac moleste
ridentem catuli ore Gallicani.
circumsistite eam et reflagitate: 10
'moecha putida, redde codicillos!
redde, putida moecha, codicillos!'
non assis facit. o lutum, lupanar,
aut si perditius potest quid esse.
sed non est tamen hoc satis putandum.   15
quod si non aliud potest, ruborem
ferreo canis exprimamus ore.
conclamate iterum altiore uoce:
'moecha putida, redde codicillos!
redde, putida moecha, codicillos!'   20
sed nil proficimus, nihil mouetur.
mutanda est ratio modusque uobis,
siquid proficere amplius potestis:
'pudica et proba, redde codicillos!'

XLIII

Salue, nec minimo puella naso
nec bello pede nec nigris ocellis
nec longis digitis nec ore sicco
nec sane nimis elegante lingua,
decoctoris amica Formiani.   5

Friend of the bankrupt from Formiae.
Kinsfolk responsible for her,   5
Call friends and doctors to advise.
The girl's not well and will not ask
For brass reflecting her true self.

XLII

Come, Hendecasyllables, one and all,
From everywhere, every one and all,
An ugly adulteress thinks I'm a joke
And refuses to give me our notebook back,
If you're prepared to stand for that.   5
Let's chase her and demand it back.
You ask which she is? You see that one
With the ugly walk and the odious actressy
Laugh and the face like a Gallican puppy's?
Surround her and demand it back: 10
'Dirty adulteress, give back the notebook!
Give back the notebook, dirty adulteress!'
She doesn't care tuppence, the filthy trollop
Or whatever's more depraved than that.
But let's not think that we've done enough.   15
If nothing else we ought to be able
To force a blush from that brazen bitch-face.
All shout again *fortissimo*:
'Dirty adulteress, give back the notebook!
Give back the notebook, dirty adulteress!'   20
We're getting nowhere; she's quite unmoved.
You'll need to change your tone and tactics
To find if you're able to get any further:
'Virtuous Lady, the notebook, please!'

XLIII

Greetings, girl with no mini nose
Nor pretty foot nor dark eyes
Nor long fingers nor dry mouth
Nor altogether felicitous tongue,
Friend of the bankrupt from Formiae.   5

ten Prouincia narrat esse bellam?
tecum Lesbia nostra comparatur?
o saeclum insapiens et infacetum!

XLIV

O Funde noster seu Sabine seu Tiburs
(nam te esse Tiburtem autumant quibus non est
cordi Catullum laedere, at quibus cordi est
quouis Sabinum pignore esse contendunt),
sed seu Sabine siue uerius Tiburs,   5
fui libenter in tua suburbana
uilla malamque pectore expuli tussim
non immerenti quam mihi meus uenter,
dum sumptuosas appeto, dedit, cenas.
nam Sestianus dum uolo esse conuiua,   10
orationem in Antium petitorem
plenam ueneni et pestilentiae legi.
hic me grauedo frigida et frequens tussis
quassauit usque dum in tuum sinum fugi
et me recuraui otioque et urtica.   15
quare refectus maximas tibi grates
ago, meum quod non es ultu' peccatum.
nec deprecor iam, si nefaria scripta
Sesti recepso, quin grauedinem et tussim
non mi sed ipsi Sestio ferat frigus,   20
qui tunc uocat me cum malum librum legi.

XLV

Acmen Septimius, suos amores,
tenens in gremio 'mea' inquit 'Acme,
ni te perdite amo atque amare porro
omnes sum assidue paratus annos
quantum qui pote plurimum perire,   5
solus in Libya Indiaque tosta
cacsio ueniam obuius leoni.'
hoc ut dixit, Amor sinistra ut ante
dextra sternuit approbationem.

And does the Province call you pretty?
Compare our Lesbia to you?
O what tasteless boorish times!

XLIV

Our Farm, which art or Sabine or Tiburtan
(For whoso have no heart to hurt Catullus
Dub thee Tiburtan, whereas whoso do
Will wager anything that Thou art Sabine),
But whether Sabine or in truth Tiburtan,   5
Right gladly have I been in Thy suburban
Villa and rid my chest of a bad cough
Not undeservedly upon me brought
For coveting rich dinners by my belly.
For while I wanted to be Sestius' guest   10
I read his speech on Antius' candidacy,
Speech packed with poison and with pestilence,
Whereat a feverish cold and chronic cough
Kept shaking me till I fled to Thy bosom
And cured me there with idleness and nettle.   15
Wherefore restored I render Thee great thanks
Because Thou didst not punish my offence,
Nor do I now object, should I accept
Sestius' vile works, if their frigidity
Give Sestius, not me, a cold and cough,   20
Whose invitation means reading bad books.

XLV

Septimius, his belovèd Acme
In his lap, said 'Acme darling,
If I'm not desperately in love
And set to go on loving you
Forever in utter desperation,   5
Then lone in Libya or scorched India
I'll face a lion with green eyes.'
At this Love sneezed, first on the right,
Then on the left, approvingly.

at Acme, leuiter caput reflectens   10
et dulcis pueri ebrios ocellos
illo purpureo ore suauiata,
'sic,' inquit 'mea uita Septimille,
huic uni domino usque seruiamus
ut multo mihi maior acriorque   15
ignis mollibus ardet in medullis.'
hoc ut dixit, Amor sinistra ut ante
dextra sternuit approbationem.
nunc ab auspicio bono profecti
mutuis animis amant amantur.   20
unam Septimius misellus Acmen
mauult quam Syrias Britanniasque;
uno in Septimio fidelis Acme
facit delicias libidinesque.
quis ullos homines beatiores   25
uidit, quis Venerem auspicatiorem?

XLVI

Iam uer egelidos refert tepores,
iam caeli furor aequinoctialis
iucundis Zephyri silescit aureis.
linquantur Phrygii, Catulle, campi
Nicaeaeque ager uber aestuosae.   5
ad claras Asiae uolemus urbes.
iam mens praetrepidans auet uagari,
iam laeti studio pedes uigescunt.
o dulces comitum ualete coetus,
longe quos simul a domo profectos   10
diuersae uarie uiae reportant.

XLVII

Porci et Socration, duae sinistrae
Pisonis, scabies famesque mundi,
uos Veraniolo meo et Fabullo
uerpus praeposuit Priapus ille?
uos conuiuia lauta sumptuose   5
de die facitis, mei sodales
quaerunt in triuio uocationes?

But Acme, lightly tilting back   10
Her head and kissing her sweet boy's
Drunken eyes with that rosy mouth,
Said 'Septimillus, so, my life,
May we always serve this one master
Surely as burns in my soft marrow   15
A bigger far and fiercer fire.'
At this Love sneezed, first on the right,
Then on the left, approvingly.
Now, setting out from this good omen,
With mutual minds they're loved and love.   20
Poor Septimius prefers his Acme
To all the Syrias and Britains.
Faithful Acme in her Septimius
Finds all desires and delights.
Who has seen any happier people?   25
Who a Venus more starry-eyed?

XLVI

Now spring brings back unfrozen warmth,
Now the sky's equinoctial fury
Is hushed by Zephyr's welcome airs.
Take leave of Phrygian plains, Catullus,
And sweltering Nicaea's lush fields.   5
Let's fly to Asia's famous cities.
Excited thoughts now long to travel;
Glad feet now tap in expectation.
Farewell, sweet company of comrades,
Who leaving distant home together   10
Return by different routes apart.

XLVII

Socration and Porcius, Piso's pair
Of left-hand men, the world's Itch and Greed,
That docked Priapus prefers you
To my Verániolus and Fabullus?
Do you throw smart expensive parties   5
All day long, while my companions
Tout in the streets for invitations?

XLVIII

Mellitos oculos tuos, Iuuenti,
siquis me sinat usque basiare,
usque ad milia basiem trecenta
nec numquam uidear satur futurus,
non si densior aridis aristis   5
sit nostrae seges osculationis.

XLIX

Disertissime Romuli nepotum,
quot sunt quotque fuere, Marce Tulli,
quotque post aliis erunt in annis,
gratias tibi maximas Catullus
agit pessimus omnium poeta,   5
tanto pessimus omnium poeta
quanto tu optimus omnium patronus.

L

Hesterno, Licini, die otiosi
multum lusimus in meis tabellis,
ut conuenerat esse delicatos.
scribens uersiculos uterque nostrum
ludebat numero modo hoc modo illoc,   5
reddens mutua per iocum atque uinum.
atque illinc abii tuo lepore
incensus, Licini, facetiisque,
ut nec me miserum cibus iuuaret
nec somnus tegeret quiete ocellos,   10
sed toto indomitus furore lecto
uersarer, cupiens uidere lucem,
ut tecum loquerer simulque ut essem.
at dcfcssa labore membra postquam
semimortua lectulo iacebant,   15
hoc, iucunde, tibi poema feci,
ex quo perspiceres meum dolorem.

XLVIII

Your honeyed eyes, Juventius,
If someone let me go on kissing,
I'd kiss three hundred thousand times
Nor never think I'd had enough,
Not if our osculation's crop   5
Were closer-packed than dried corn-ears.

XLIX

Most eloquent of Romulus' grandsons
That are and have been, Marcus Tullius,
And ever will be in other years,
Catullus, the worst poet of all,
Sends you herewith his greatest thanks,   5
As truly the worst poet of all
As you're best advocate of all.

L

At leisure, Licinius, yesterday
We'd much fun with my writing-tablets
As we'd agreed to be frivolous.
Each of us writing light verses
Played now with this metre, now that,   5
Capping each other's jokes and toasts.
Yes, and I left there fired by
Your charm, Licinius, and wit,
So food gave poor me no pleasure
Nor could I rest my eyes in sleep   10
But wildly excited turned and tossed
Over the bed, longing for daylight
That I might be with you and talk.
But after my tired aching limbs
Were lying on the couch half dead,   15
I made this poem for you, the charmer,
So you could spot my trouble from it.

nunc audax caue sis, precesque nostras,
oramus, caue despuas, ocelle,
ne poenas Nemesis reposcat a te.   20
est uemens Dea; laedere hanc caueto.

LI

Ille mi par esse Deo uidetur,
ille, si fas est, superare Diuos,
qui sedens aduersus identidem te
spectat et audit

dulce ridentem, misero quod omnis   5
eripit sensus mihi. nam simul te,
Lesbia, aspexi, nihil est super mi
⟨uocis in ore,⟩

lingua sed torpet, tenuis sub artus
flamma demanat, sonitu suopte   10
tintinant aures, gemina teguntur
lumina nocte.

otium, Catulle, tibi molestum est.
otio exsultas nimiumque gestis.
otium et reges prius et beatas   15
perdidit urbes.

LII

Quid est, Catulle? quid moraris emori?
sella in curuli struma Nonius sedet;
per consulatum peierat Vatinius.
quid est, Catulle? quid moraris emori?

LIII

Risi nescioquem modo e corona
qui, cum mirifice Vatiniana
meus crimina Caluos explicasset,
admirans ait haec manusque tollens:
'Di magni, salaputium disertum!'   5

Now don't be rash, please—don't reject
Our prayers, we implore you, precious,
Lest Nemesis make you pay for it.   20
She's a drastic Goddess. Don't provoke her.

LI

That man is seen by me as a God's equal
Or (if it may be said) the Gods' superior,
Who sitting opposite again and again
Watches and hears *you*

Sweetly laughing—which dispossesses poor me   5
Of all my senses, for no sooner, Lesbia,
Do I look at you than there's no power left me
⟨Of speech in my mouth,⟩

But my tongue's paralysed, invisible flame
Courses down through my limbs, with din of their own   10
My ears are ringing and twin darkness covers
The light of my eyes.

Leisure, Catullus, does not agree with you.
At leisure you're restless, too excitable.
Leisure in the past has ruined rulers and   15
Prosperous cities.

LII

What next, Catullus? Why defer decease?
Nonius the tumour sits in curule state,
Vatinius by his consulate's forsworn.
What next, Catullus? Why defer decease?

LIII

I laughed at someone in court lately
Who, when my Calvus gave a splendid
Account of all Vatinius' crimes,
With hands raised in surprise announced
'Great Gods, the squirt's articulate!'   5

LIV

Othonis caput (oppido est pusillum)
et, trirustice, semilauta crura,
subtile et leue peditum Libonis,
si non omnia, displicere uellem
tibi et Fuficio seni recocto.   5
irascere iterum meis iambis
immerentibus, unice imperator.

LV

Oramus, si forte non molestum est,
demonstres ubi sint tuae tenebrae.
te in Campo quaesiuimus minore,
te in Circo, te in omnibus libellis,
te in templo summi Iouis sacrato.   5
in Magni simul ambulatione
femellas omnes, amice, prendi,
quas uultu uidi tamen sereno.
'a, cette huc' sic usque flagitabam
'Camerium mihi, pessimae puellae.'   10
'en' inquit quaedam, sinum reducens,
'en hic in roseis latet papillis.'
sed te iam ferre Herculei labos est;
tanto te in fastu negas, amice.
dic nobis ubi sis futurus, ede   15
audacter, committe, crede luci.
nunc te lacteolae tenent puellae?
si linguam clauso tenes in ore,
fructus proicies amoris omnes.
ucrbosa gaudet Venus loquella.   20
uel, si uis, licet obseres palatum,
dum uestri sim particeps amoris.

LVI

O rem ridiculam, Cato, et iocosam
dignamque auribus et tuo cachinno!
ride quidquid amas, Cato, Catullum.

LIV

Otho's head (it's mighty weak)
And, you hick, his half-washed legs,
Libo's soft and wily fart,
These at least I could wish displeased
You and old warmed-up Fuficius.   5
Once more my innocuous iambics
Will rile you, Generalissimo.

LV

We beg you, meaning no offence,
To show us where your hide-out is.
We've sought you in the lesser Campus,
In the Circus, in all the bookshops,
In the hallowed shrine of Jove Most High.   5
At the same time in Magnus' Walk
I seized on all the girlies, friend,
Although I saw they looked quite cool.
'Hand him over!' I kept demanding,
'I want Camerius, naughty girls.'   10
'Look,' said one, drawing back her dress,
'He's hiding here—on rosy nipples.'
But enduring you now is a labour of Hercules;
Your absence, friend, is so arrogant.
Tell us where you'll be, speak out   15
Boldly, share it, trust the light.
Are milk-white girls now holding you?
If you shut your mouth and hold your tongue
You'll throw away all the fruits of love.
Venus loves volubility.   20
Or if you like you may seal your lips
Provided I can share your love.

LVI

O a funny thing, Cato, quite absurd,
Worth your hearing and chuckling over.
Laugh as you love Catullus, Cato.

res est ridicula et nimis iocosa.
deprendi modo pupulum puellae   5
trusantem; hunc ego, si placet Dionae,
protelo rigida mea cecidi.

LVII

Pulcre conuenit improbis cinaedis,
Mamurrae pathicoque Caesarique.
nec mirum. maculae pares utrisque,
urbana altera et illa Formiana,
impressae resident nec cluentur.   5
morbosi pariter, gemelli utrique,
uno in lectulo erudituli ambo,
non hic quam ille magis uorax adulter,
riuales socii puellularum.
pulcre conuenit improbis cinaedis.   10

LVIII

Caeli, Lesbia nostra, Lesbia illa,
illa Lesbia quam Catullus unam
plus quam se atque suos amauit omnes,
nunc in quadriuiis et angiportis
glubit magnanimi Remi nepotes.   5

LVIII B

Non custos si fingar ille Cretum,
non Ladas ego pinnipesue Perseus,   3
non si Pegaseo ferar uolatu,   2
non Rhesi niueae citaeque bigae;
adde huc plumipedas uolatilesque,   5
uentorumque simul require cursum,
quos iunctos, Cameri, mihi dicares,
defessus tamen omnibus medullis
et multis languoribus peresus
essem te, mi amice, quaeritando.   10

The thing's too funny, quite absurd.
I lately caught the girl's boy pet   5
Wanking, and (so please Dione!)
Banged him in tandem with my hard.

LVII

They're a fine match, the shameless sods,
Those poofters Caesar and Mamurra.
No wonder. Equivalent black marks,
One urban, the other Formian,
Are stamped indelibly on each.   5
Diseased alike, both didymous,
Two sciolists on one wee couch,
Peers in adultery and greed,
Rival mates among the nymphets,
They're a fine match, the shameless sods.   10

LVIII

Caelius, our Lesbia, *the* Lesbia,
The Lesbia whom alone Catullus
Loved more than self and all his kin,
At crossroads now and in back alleys
Peels great-hearted Remus' grandsons.   5

LVIII B

Not if I were Crete's fabled guard
Or Ladas or wing-footed Perseus,
Not if I flew on Pegasus
Or Rhesus' swift and snow-white pair;
To these add feather-feet and fliers   5
And ask too for the speed of winds—
Hand me these harnessed, Camerius,
I'd still be worn down to the marrow
And eaten up with lassitude
In the long search for you, my friend.   10

LIX

Bononiensis Rufa Rufulum fellat,
uxor Meneni, saepe quam in sepulcretis
uidistis ipso rapere de rogo cenam,
cum deuolutum ex igne prosequens panem
ab semiraso tunderetur ustore.   5

LX

Num te leaena montibus Libystinis
aut Scylla latrans infima inguinum parte
tam mente dura procreauit ac taetra
ut supplicis uocem in nouissimo casu
contemptam haberes, a, nimis fero corde?   5

LXI

Collis o Heliconii
cultor, Vraniae genus,
qui rapis teneram ad uirum
uirginem, o Hymenaee Hymen,
o Hymen Hymenaee,   5

cinge tempora floribus
suaue olentis amaraci,
flammeum cape laetus, huc
huc ueni, niueo gerens
luteum pede soccum;   10

excitusque hilari die,
nuptialia concinens
uoce carmina tinnula,
pelle humum pedibus, manu
pineam quate taedam.   15

namque Iunia Manlio,
qualis Idalium colens
uenit ad Phrygium Venus
iudicem, bona cum bona
nubet alite uirgo,   20

LIX

Bononian Rufa sucks off Rufulus—
Menenius' wife, whom you have often seen
In graveyards grabbing dinner from a pyre,
Chasing a loaf that's rolled down from the flames,
Knocked off meanwhile by the half-shaven cremator.   5

LX

Did lioness among Libystine mountains
Or Scylla barking from groin's lowest part
Produce you with a mind so hard and horrid
That you could spurn in his extremest need
A suppliant's prayer, ah too cruel-hearted?   5

LXI

O you dweller on the hill
Of Helicon, Urania's breed,
You who kidnap tender bride
For groom, O Hymeneal Hymen,
O Hymen Hymeneal,   5

Wreathe your temples with the flower
Of sweet-smelling marjoram;
Take the flame-hued veil and gladly
Hither come, on snow-white foot
Wearing yellow sandal.   10

Excited by the merry day,
With ringing tenor voice join in
The wedding chorus, beat the ground
With dancing feet and in your hand
Shake the torch of pinewood.   15

For Junia, as beautiful
As Idalium's mistress
Venus coming to the Phrygian
Judge, is wedding Manlius,
Good maiden with good omen,   20

floridis uelut enitens
myrtus Asia ramulis
quos Hamadryades Deae
ludicrum sibi roscido
nutriunt umore.   25

quare age, huc aditum ferens,
perge linquere Thespiae
rupis Aonios specus,
nympha quos super irrigat
frigerans Aganippe,   30

ac domum dominam uoca
coniugis cupidam noui,
mentem amore reuinciens
ut tenax hedera huc et huc
arborem implicat errans.   35

uosque item simul, integrae
uirgines, quibus aduenit
par dies, agite in modum
dicite 'o Hymenaee Hymen,
o Hymen Hymenaee',   40

ut lubentius, audiens
se citarier ad suum
munus, huc aditum ferat
dux bonae Veneris, boni
coniugator amoris.   45

quis Deus magis est ama-
tis petendus amantibus?
quem colent homines magis
Caelitum, o Hymenaee Hymen,
o Hymen Hymenaee?   50

te suis tremulus parens
inuocat, tibi uirgines
zonula soluunt sinus,
te timens cupida nouos
captat aure maritus.   55

Like an Asian myrtle-bush
Shining bright with flowering twigs,
Which Hamadryad Goddesses
Nourish with the drops of dew
As their own plaything.   25

Come then, making your approach
Here, and quit the Aonian
Grottoes of the Thespian rock,
Which the cool Nymph Aganippe
Waters from above.   30

To her home invite the mistress
Hungry for her new husband,
Wrapping her mind round with love
As clinging ivy entwines the tree,
Roving here and there.   35

And you too at the same time,
Unwed maidens, for whom comes
A like day, in tune and rhythm
Sing 'O Hymeneal Hymen,
O Hymen Hymeneal',   40

So that the more gladly, hearing
Himself summoned to his proper
Duty, he may make approach here
As the bringer of good Venus
And good love's uniter.   45

Is any God more to be sought
After by belovèd lovers?
Which Heavenly One will humans sooner
Worship, O Hymeneal Hymen,
O Hymen Hymeneal?   50

The trembling parent prays to you
For his children, virgins loose
The girdle of their dress for you,
And for you the scared new husband
Listens with keen ear.   55

tu fero iuueni in manus
floridam ipse puellulam
dedis a gremio suae
matris, o Hymenaee Hymen,
o Hymen Hymenaee.   60

nil potest sine te Venus,
fama quod bona comprobet,
commodi capere, at potest
te uolente. quis huic Deo
compararier ausit?   65

nulla quit sine te domus
liberos dare, nec parens
stirpe nitier, at potest
te uolente. quis huic Deo
compararier ausit?   70

quae tuis careat sacris
non queat dare praesides
terra finibus, at queat
te uolente. quis huic Deo
compararier ausit?   75

claustra pandite ianuae.
uirgo, ades. uiden ut faces
splendidas quatiunt comas?
. . . . .
. . . . .
. . . . .
. . . . .

tardet ingenuus pudor;
quem tamen magis audiens   80
flet quod ire necesse est.

flere desine. non tibi, Au-
runculeia, periculum est
ne qua femina pulcrior
clarum ab Oceano diem   85
uiderit uenientem.

Into the hands of a rough youth
From the bosom of her mother
You commit a bride in tender
Bloom, O Hymeneal Hymen,
O Hymen Hymeneal.   60

Without you Venus can gain
No advantage good repute
Would approve of, but she can
With your favour. Who would dare
Compare with this God?   65

Without you no house can have
Free-born children and no parent
Depend on offspring, but they can
With your favour. Who would dare
Compare with this God?   70

Any land without your rites
Cannot produce guardians
Of its borders, but it can
With your favour. Who would dare
Compare with this God?   75

Unbar and open wide the door.
Maiden, come. Look how the torches
Toss their shining hair about

              . . . . .

              . . . . .

              . . . . .

Free-born modesty delays;
Which, though, heeding all the more   80
She weeps at having to go.

Cease weeping. Not for you, Aurun-
culeia, is there risk at all
That any woman lovelier
Has ever watched the light of day   85
Coming from the Ocean.

talis in uario solet
diuitis domini hortulo
stare flos hyacinthinus.
sed moraris, abit dies;   90
prodeas, noua nupta.

prodeas, noua nupta, si
iam uidetur, et audias
nostra uerba. uiden? faces
aureas quatiunt comas.   95
prodeas, noua nupta.

non tuus leuis in mala
deditus uir adultera,
probra turpia persequens,
a tuis teneris uolet   100
secubare papillis,

lenta sed uelut adsitas
uitis implicat arbores,
implicabitur in tuum
complexum. sed abit dies;   105
prodeas, noua nupta.

o cubile quod omnibus
. . . . .
. . . . .
. . . . .

candido pede lecti,

quae tuo ueniunt ero,
quanta gaudia, quae uaga   110
nocte, quae medio die
gaudeat! sed abit dies;
prodeas, noua nupta.

tollite, o pueri, faces;
flammeum uideo uenire.   115
ite concinite in modum
'io Hymen Hymenaee io,
io Hymen Hymenaee.'

Just so in the variety
Of a rich owner's garden plot
The hyacinth in flower stands out.
But you delay and day goes by.   90
Please come out, new bride.

Please come out, new bride, if now
You are ready, and listen to
Our words. Do you see? The torches
Toss their golden hair about.   95
Please come out, new bride.

Your husband is not light, not tied
To some bad adulteress,
Nor pursuing shameful scandal
Will he wish to sleep apart   100
From your tender nipples,

But, just as the limber vine
Enfolds trees planted beside it,
He will be enfolded in
Your embrace. But day goes by;   105
Please come out, new bride.

O bed, which for everyone
          . . . . .
          . . . . .
          . . . . .
By the couch's white foot,

What joys are coming to your lord!
What great joys for him to enjoy   110
In the wanton night and at
Midday too! But day goes by;
Please come out, new bride.

Raise the torches high, O boys.
I see the flame-hued veil approach.   115
Come now, sing together in tune
'O Hymen Hymeneal O,
O Hymen Hymeneal.'

ne diu taceat procax
Fescennina iocatio,　　　　　　　　　　120
nec nuces pueris neget
desertum domini audiens
concubinus amorem.

da nuces pueris, iners
concubine. satis diu　　　　　　　　　125
lusisti nucibus. lubet
iam seruire Talassio.
concubine, nuces da.

sordebant tibi uilicae,
concubine, hodie atque heri.　　　　　130
nunc tuum cinerarius
tondet os. miser a miser
concubine, nuces da.

diceris male te a tuis
unguentate glabris marite　　　　　　135
abstinere, sed abstine.
io Hymen Hymenaee io,
io Hymen Hymenaee.

scimus haec tibi quae licent
sola cognita, sed marito　　　　　　　140
ista non eadem licent.
io Hymen Hymenace io,
io Hymen Hymenaee.

nupta, tu quoque quae tuus
uir petet caue ne neges,　　　　　　　145
ne petitum aliunde eat.
io Hymen Hymenaee io,
io Hymen Hymenaee.

en tibi domus ut potens
et beata uiri tui!　　　　　　　　　　150
quae tibi sine seruiat—
io Hymen Hymenaee io,
io Hymen Hymenaee—

Let the ribald Fescennine
Jesting not be silent longer   120
Nor boy concubine refuse
Nuts to the children when he hears
Of master's love abandoned.

Give the children nuts, you idle
Concubine. For long enough   125
You have played with nuts, but now
It's time to serve Talassius.
Concubine, give nuts.

Today and yesterday you scorned
The home-farm women, concubine.   130
Now, however, the *friseur*
Shaves your cheek. Ah, poor, poor thing!
Concubine, give nuts.

You are said to find it hard,
Perfumed bridegroom, to give up   135
Smooth-skinned boys, but give them up,
O Hymen Hymeneal O,
O Hymen Hymeneal.

We realize you've only known
Permitted pleasures; husbands, though,   140
Have no right to the same pleasures.
O Hymen Hymeneal O,
O Hymen Hymeneal.

You too, bride, beware of not
Giving your man all he asks,   145
Lest he go elsewhere to ask.
O Hymen Hymeneal O,
O Hymen Hymeneal.

Here is home for you, your man's
(Look how powerful and blest!)   150
Which you must allow to serve you
(O Hymen Hymeneal O,
O Hymen Hymeneal)

usque dum tremulum mouens
cana tempus anilitas   155
omnia omnibus annuit.
io Hymen Hymenaee io,
io Hymen Hymenaee.

transfer omine cum bono
limen aureolos pedes,   160
rasilemque subi forem.
io Hymen Hymenaee io,
io Hymen Hymenaee.

aspice intus ut accubans
uir tuus Tyrio in toro   165
totus immineat tibi.
io Hymen Hymenaee io,
io Hymen Hymenaee.

illi non minus ac tibi
pectore uritur intimo   170
flamma, sed penite magis.
io Hymen Hymenaee io,
io Hymen Hymenaee.

mitte bracchiolum teres,
praetextate, puellulae.   175
iam cubile adeat uiri.
io Hymen Hymenaee io,
io Hymen Hymenaee.

uos, bonae senibus uiris
cognitae bene feminae,   180
collocate puellulam.
io Hymen Hymenaee io,
io Hymen Hymenaee.

iam licet uenias, marite.
uxor in thalamo tibi est,   185
ore floridulo nitens,
alba parthenice uelut
luteumue papauer.

Till white-haired old-womanhood
With ever nodding head agrees   155
With everyone on everything.
O Hymen Hymeneal O,
O Hymen Hymeneal.

Lift your little golden feet
With good omen over the   160
Threshold, past the polished door.
O Hymen Hymeneal O,
O Hymen Hymeneal.

Look inside, how lying there
Your man on the Tyrian couch   165
Is totally intent on you.
O Hymen Hymeneal O,
O Hymen Hymeneal.

For him no less than for you
In his inner self there burns   170
A fire, but more inwardly.
O Hymen Hymeneal O,
O Hymen Hymeneal.

Let go the slender little arm
Of the girl-bride, *praetexta*'d page.   175
Now she should approach her man's bed.
O Hymen Hymeneal O,
O Hymen Hymeneal.

You, good women well and truly
Known to your elderly men,   180
Settle the girl-bride in her place.
O Hymen Hymeneal O,
O Hymen Hymeneal.

And now, bridegroom, you may come.
Your wife is in the bridal chamber,   185
Her face shining like a floret,
Like the white parthenium
Or the yellow poppy.

at, marite, ita me iuuent
Caelites, nihilo minus   190
pulcer es, neque te Venus
neglegit. sed abit dies;
perge, ne remorare.

non diu remoratus es.
iam uenis. bona te Venus   195
iuuerit, quoniam palam
quod cupis cupis, et bonum
non abscondis amorem.

ille pulueris Africi
siderumque micantium   200
subducat numerum prius,
qui uestri numerare uolt
multa milia ludi.

ludite ut lubet, et breui
liberos date. non decet   205
tam uetus sine liberis
nomen esse, sed indidem
semper ingenerari.

Torquatus uolo paruulus
matris e gremio suae   210
porrigens teneras manus
dulce rideat ad patrem
semihiante labello.

sit suo similis patri
Manlio, et facile insciis   215
noscitetur ab obuiis,
et pudicitiam suae
matris indicet ore.

talis illius a bona
matre laus genus approbet   220
qualis unica ab optima
matre Telemacho manet
fama Penelopeo.

But, so help me Heaven-Dwellers,
Bridegroom, you are none the less　　　190
Beautiful. Venus has not
Forgotten you. But day goes by;
Come on, do not linger.

No, you have not lingered long.
Now you're coming. May good Venus　　195
Help you, as it's obvious
You desire what you desire
And aren't hiding good love.

Let him first work out the number
Of the dust of Africa　　　　　　　200
And the twinkling stars above
Whoever wants to number your
Many thousand love-games.

Play as you please and very soon
Produce children. It's not right　　　205
That so old a name should lack
Children, but from the same stock
It should ever sire them.

I want a miniature Torquatus
From the bosom of his mother　　　210
Stretching out his tender hands
To smile sweetly at his father,
Little lips half-parted.

May he look like Manlius
His father, recognizable　　　　　215
By those he meets not in the know
And by his features demonstrate
His mother's chastity.

May his praise be evidence
Of descent from a good mother,　　　220
Just as from Penelope,
Best of mothers, peerless fame
Lasts for Telemachus.

claudite ostia, uirgines.
lusimus satis. at boni 225
coniuges, bene uiuite et
munere assiduo ualentem
exercete iuuentam.

LXII

Vesper adest, iuuenes, consurgite; Vesper Olympo
expectata diu uix tandem lumina tollit.
surgere iam tempus, iam pinguis linquere mensas;
iam ueniet uirgo, iam dicetur Hymenaeus.
  Hymen o Hymenaee, Hymen ades o Hymenaee! 5

Cernitis, innuptae, iuuenes? consurgite contra.
nimirum Oetaeos ostendit Noctifer ignes.
sic certest. uiden ut perniciter exsiluere?
non temere exsiluere; canent quod uincere par
    est.
  Hymen o Hymenaee, Hymen ades o Hymenaee! 10

Non facilis nobis, aequales, palma parata est.
aspicite innuptae secum ut meditata requirunt.
non frustra meditantur; habent memorabile quod
    sit.
nec mirum, penitus quae tota mente laborant.
nos alio mentes, alio diuisimus
    aures. 15
iure igitur uincemur; amat uictoria curam.
quare nunc animos saltem conuertite uestros.
dicere iam incipient, iam respondere decebit.
  Hymen o Hymenaee, Hymen ades o Hymenaee!

Hespere, quis caelo fertur crudelior ignis? 20
qui natam possis complexu auellere matris,
complexu matris retinentem auellere natam,
et iuueni ardenti castam donare puellam.
quid faciunt hostes capta crudelius urbe?
  Hymen o Hymenaee, Hymen ades o Hymenaee! 25

Close the doors, unmarried girls.
We have played enough. But you,   225
Good wedded couple, live well and
Exercise your lusty youth
In its constant duty.

LXII

Vesper is here, young men; stand up. Vesper at last
Is lifting on Olympus his long-awaited light.
Time now to stand up, time to leave the laden tables.
Now comes the bride, now Hymeneal will be sung.
    Hymen O Hymeneal, Hymen come, O Hymeneal!   5

You see the young men, maidens? Stand up opposite.
Night's herald must be showing his Oetéan fires.
Yes, certainly. You saw how quickly they jumped up?
They jumped up with good reason; their song's likely
    to win.
    Hymen O Hymeneal, Hymen come, O Hymeneal!   10

No easy palm is waiting for us, my compeers.
Look how the girls are practising their piece together.
Their practice isn't wasted; they've something
    memorable.
No wonder; all their thoughts are on the work in hand.
But we've been hearing one thing and thinking of
    another.   15
It's right we should be losers; victory takes pains.
So now for once begin to concentrate your minds.
They'll soon be singing; soon we'll have to answer them.
    Hymen O Hymeneal, Hymen come, O Hymeneal!

Hesperus, what fire more cruel rides the sky?   20
For you can tear a daughter from her mother's arms,
From her mother's arms can tear a clinging daughter
And hand a chaste girl over to an ardent youth.
On a town's capture what more cruel can foes do?
    Hymen O Hymeneal, Hymen come, O Hymeneal!   25

Hespere, quis caelo lucet iucundior ignis?
qui desponsa tua firmes conubia flamma
quae pepigere uiri, pepigerunt ante parentes,
nec iunxere prius quam se tuus extulit ardor.
quid datur a Diuis felici optatius hora? 30
   Hymen o Hymenaee, Hymen ades o Hymenaee!
Hesperus e nobis, aequales, abstulit unam
     . . . .

     . . . .

namque tuo aduentu uigilat custodia semper.
nocte latent fures, quos idem sacpc reuertens,
Hespere, mutato comprendis nomine Eous. 35
at lubet innuptis ficto te carpere questu.
quid tum, si carpunt tacita quem mente requirunt?
   Hymen o Hymenaee, Hymen ades o Hymenaee!
Vt flos in saeptis secretus nascitur hortis,
ignotus pecori, nullo conuolsus aratro, 40
quem mulcent aurae, firmat sol, educat imber;
multi illum pueri, multae optauere puellae:
idem cum tenui carptus defloruit ungui,
nulli illum pueri, nullae optauere puellae:
sic uirgo, dum intacta manet, dum cara suis est; 45
cum castum amisit polluto corpore
   florem,
nec pueris iucunda manet nec cara puellis.
   Hymen o Hymenaee, Hymen ades o Hymenaee!
Vt uidua in nudo uitis quae nascitur aruo
numquam se extollit, numquam mitem educat uuam, 50
sed tenerum prono deflectens pondere corpus
iam iam contingit summum radice flagellum;
hanc nulli agricolae, nulli coluere iuuenci:
at si forte eadem est ulmo coniuncta marito,
multi illam agricolae, multi coluere iuuenci: 55
sic uirgo, dum intacta manet, dum inculta
   senescit;
cum par conubium maturo temporc adcpta est,
cara uiro magis et minus est inuisa parenti.

Hesperus, what fire more pleasing lights the sky?
For with your flame you ratify the marriage promise
Which parents pledge beforehand and fiancés pledge
But don't fulfil until your ardent self appears.
What can Gods give more welcome than the happy hour?   30
   Hymen O Hymeneal, Hymen come, O Hymeneal!

Hesperus, my compeers, has kidnapped one of us.

. . . .

. . . .

For always at your coming watchmen go on duty.
Thieves can hide at night, but you at dawn returning,
Hesperus, often catch them, known then as Eous.   35
Maidens enjoy attacking you with false complaints.
What of it? They attack but secretly they want you.
   Hymen O Hymeneal, Hymen come O Hymeneal!

Just as a flower that grows in a garden close, apart,
Unbeknown to sheep, not torn up by the plough,   40
Which breezes fondle, the sun strengthens, showers feed;
Many boys have longed for it and many girls:
But when its bloom is gone, nipped off by a fingernail,
Never boy has longed for it and never girl:
A maid too while untouched is dear the while to kin;   45
But when with body smirched she loses her chaste
      bloom,
She's neither pleasing then to boys nor dear to girls.
   Hymen O Hymeneal, Hymen come, O Hymeneal!

Just as the unwed vine that grows on naked ground
Can never raise herself, never produce ripe grapes,   50
But bending down frail body under her prone weight
With topmost tendril's tip can almost touch her root;
Never has farmer tended her and never oxen:
But if she happens to be joined to a husband elm,
Then many farmers, many oxen have tended her: 55
A maid too while untouched grows old the while
      untended,
But when in due time she has made an equal marriage,
She's dearer to a man and less trying to parents.

Et tu ne pugna cum tali coniuge, uirgo.
non aequom est pugnare pater cui tradidit ipse,   60
ipse pater cum matre, quibus parere necesse
    est.
uirginitas non tota tua est, ex parte parentum
    est;
tertia pars patrist, pars est data tertia matri,
tertia sola tua est. noli pugnare duobus
qui genero sua iura simul cum dote dederunt.   65
    Hymen o Hymenaee, Hymen ades o Hymenaee!

LXIII

Super alta uectus Attis celeri rate maria,
Phrygium ut nemus citato cupide pede
    tetigit
adiitque opaca siluis redimita loca Deae,
stimulatus ibi furenti rabie, uagus animis,
deuolsit ili acuto sibi pondera silice.   5
itaque ut relicta sensit sibi membra sine
    uiro,
etiam recente terrae sola sanguine maculans,
niueis citata cepit manibus leue
    typanum,
typanum tuum, Cybebe, tua, mater, initia,
quatiensque terga tauri teneris caua digitis   10
canere haec suis adorta est tremebunda comitibus:
'agite ite ad alta, Gallae, Cybeles nemora
    simul,
simul ite, Dindymenae Dominae uaga pecora,
aliena quae petentes uelut exules loca
sectam meam exsecutae duce me mihi comites   15
rapidum salum tulistis truculentaque pelagi,
et corpus euirastis Veneris nimio
    odio;
hilarate Erae citatis erroribus
    animum.
mora tarda mente cedat, simul ite, sequimini
Phrygiam ad domum Cybebes, Phrygia ad nemora
    Deae,   20

And you are not to fight with such a husband, maiden.
It is not fair to fight him to whom father gave you,   60
Father himself with mother, whom you are bound
    to obey.
Your maidenhead is not all yours but in part your
    parents';
Your father has a third, your mother is given a third,
Only a third is yours. Don't fight against the two
Who gave a son-in-law their own rights with your dowry.   65
    Hymen O Hymeneal, Hymen come O Hymeneal!

LXIII

Over the high seas Attis, carried in a speedy craft,
When he touched the grove in Phrygia eagerly with
    hurrying feet
And approached the Goddess' gloomy forest-girt domain,
There, by raving madness goaded, his wits astray,
He tore off with a sharp flint the burden of his groin.   5
Then, conscious that the members left him were now
    unmanned,
Still with fresh blood spotting the surface of the ground,
In snow-white hand she swiftly seized the light
    tambourine,
Your tambourine, Cybébe, your initiation, Mother,
And tapping hollow bull's-hide with tender fingertips,   10
Proceeded thus, aflutter, to sing to her followers:
'To the heights come quickly, Gallae, together to
    Cýbele's groves,
Together come, stray cattle of the Mistress of Dindymus,
Who like a band of exiles making for foreign lands
And following my guidance, my comrades, led by me,   15
Have borne the raging salt sea and ocean's savagery,
And through excessive hatred of Venus unmanned
    yourselves,
With your impetuous wanderings gladden the heart of
    your Queen.
Rid mind of slow reluctance, together, come, follow me
To Cybébe's home in Phrygia, to the Goddess's Phrygian
    groves,   20

ubi cymbalum sonat uox, ubi tympana
    reboant,
tibicen ubi canit Phryx curuo graue
    calamo,
ubi capita Maenades ui iaciunt hederigerae,
ubi sacra sancta acutis ululatibus agitant,
ubi sueuit illa Diuae uolitare uaga
    cohors,   25
quo nos decet citatis celerare tripudiis.'

simul haec comitibus Attis cecinit, notha mulier,
thiasus repente linguis trepidantibus
    ululat,
leue tympanum remugit, caua cymbala
    recrepant,
uiridem citus adit Idam properante pede chorus.   30
furibunda simul anhelans uaga uadit animam
    agens
comitata tympano Attis per opaca nemora dux,
ueluti iuuenca uitans onus indomita iugi;
rapidae ducem sequuntur Gallae properipedem.
itaque ut domum Cybebes tetigere
    lassulae,   35
nimio e labore somnum capiunt sine Cerere.
piger his labante languore oculos sopor operit;
abit in quiete molli rabidus furor animi.
sed ubi oris aurei Sol radiantibus oculis
lustrauit aethera album, sola dura, mare ferum,   40
pepulitque noctis umbras uegetis
    sonipedibus,
ibi Somnus excitam Attin fugiens citus abiit;
trepidante eum recepit Dea Pasithea
    sinu.
ita de quiete molli rapida sine rabie
simul ipsa pectore Attis sua facta recoluit,   45
liquidaque mente uidit sine quis ubique
    foret,
animo aestuante rusum reditum ad uada tetulit.
ibi maria uasta uisens lacrimantibus oculis
patriam allocuta maestast ita uoce miseriter:

Where rings the voice of cymbals, where tambourines are
    banged,
Where Phrygian bass-pipers drone loud on their curved
    reed,
Where ivy-bearing Maenads violently toss their heads,
Where with shrill ululations they celebrate holy rites,
Where the Goddess's wandering troupers are used to rush
    around,   25
Thither it is our duty to speed in leaping dance.'

Soon as false female Attis had sung her companions this,
Suddenly the procession shrieked with trembling
    tongues,
The light tambourine was thumping, the hollow cymbals
    clanged,
The revel rout approached green Ida on hurrying feet.   30
At the same time in wandering frenzy breathless and
    breathing hard
Attis led on, attended by drums, through gloomy groves,
Just like an untamed heifer avoiding the load of the yoke;
The hurrying Gallae follow her scurry-footed lead.
And so, when those poor tired things arrived at Cybébe's
    home,   35
After too much effort without Ceres they fall asleep.
Passive slumber covers their eyes with listlessness;
In gentle rest departed their mind's mad paroxysm.
But when the Sun with golden face and flashing eyes
Purified white aether, hard land and wild sea,   40
And drove away Night's shadows with lively clatter-
    hooves,
Then Sleep from wakened Attis departed, flying fast,
To be welcomed by the Goddess Pasithea with trembling
    breast.
So, after gentle rest-time, from frenzied madness free,
When Attis' self went over in thought what she had done   45
And in her mind saw clearly where, without what, she
    was,
She dared with spirit seething return again to the shore.
There, gazing at the lonely sea with tearful eyes,
She thus addressed with sad voice her country piteously:

'patria o mei creatrix, patria o mea
    genetrix, 50
ego quam miser relinquens, dominos ut erifugae
famuli solent, ad Idae tetuli nemora pedem,
ut aput niuem et ferarum gelida stabula
    forem
et earum omnia adirem furibunda latibula,
ubinam aut quibus locis te positam, patria, reor? 55
cupit ipsa pupula ad te sibi derigere aciem,
rabie fera carens dum brcuc tempus animus est.
egone a mea remota haec ferar in nemora domo?
patria, bonis, amicis, genitoribus abero?
abero foro, palaestra, stadio et gyminasiis? 60
miser a miser, querendum est etiam atque etiam, anime.
quod enim genus figuraest ego non quod obierim?
ego mulier, ego adolescens, ego ephebus, ego puer,
ego gymnasi fui flos, ego eram decus olei.
mihi ianuae frequentes, mihi limina
    tepida, 65
mihi floridis corollis redimita domus erat,
linquendum ubi esset orto mihi sole cubiculum.
ego nunc Deum ministra et Cybeles famula
    ferar?
ego Maenas, ego mei pars, ego uir sterilis ero?
ego uiridis algida Idae niue amicta loca colam? 70
ego uitam agam sub altis Phrygiae columinibus,
ubi cerua siluicultrix, ubi aper
    nemoriuagus?
iam iam dolet quod egi, iam iamque paenitet.'

roseis ut huic labellis sonitus citus abiit,
geminas Deorum ad aures noua nuntia referens, 75
ibi iuncta iuga resoluens Cybele leonibus
laeuumque pecoris hostem stimulans ita loquitur:
'agedum,' inquit 'age, Ferox, i, fac ut hunc furor agitet,
fac uti furoris ictu reditum in nemora
    ferat,
mea libere nimis qui fugere imperia cupit. 80
age, caede terga cauda, tua uerbera
    patere;
fac cuncta mugienti fremitu loca retonent;

'O country that gave me being, O country that gave me
    birth,   50
Whom I wretchedly leaving as runaway servants do
Their masters, to the forests of Ida brought my feet,
That I might be among snow and wild beasts' frosty
    byres,
And draw near in my madness their every lurking-place,
Where or in what quarter, my country, do I think you lie?   55
My pupils of themselves long to turn their gaze on you,
While my spirit for a short time is free of fierce mania.
Shall *I* rush to these forests far distant from my home?
Be absent from my country, possessions, parents, friends?
Absent from forum, palaestra, stadium and gymnasia?   60
Ah wretched, wretched spirit, you must forever grieve.
What kind of human figure have I not undergone?
A woman I, a young man, an ephebe I, a child.
I've been flower of the gymnasium; I was glory of the oil.
For me the doors were crowded, for me the threshold
    warm.   65
For me with flowery posies the house was garlanded
When it was time at sunrise for me to leave my bed.
Shall I now be called Gods' handmaid and Cýbele's
    serving-girl?
Am I to be a Maenad, half me, a male unmanned?
Am I to haunt green Ida's cold, snow-mantled bounds?   70
Shall I spend life beneath the high columns of Phrygia,
With the deer woodland-haunting and forest-ranging
    boar?
Now what I've done appals me; I'm sorry for it now.'
As the sound quickly issued from out her rosy lips
Bearing a new message to the twin ears of the Gods,   75
Then Cybele, unloosing the yoke that joined her lions
And pricking the kine-killer upon the left, spoke thus:
'Be off' she said, 'go, Ferox, make frenzy drive him on,
Make him retrace his footsteps to the forest frenzy-
    struck,
Who desires too freely to escape from my commands.   80
Come suffer your own lashes, flog your back with your
    tail,
Make every corner thunder again with bellowing roar;

rutilam, Ferox, torosa ceruice quate iubam.'
ait haec minax Cybebe religatque iuga
    manu.
ferus ipse sese adhortans rabidum incitat animum;   85
uadit, fremit, refringit uirgulta pede
    uago.
at ubi umida albicantis loca litoris
    adiit
teneramque uidit Attin prope marmora pelagi,
facit impetum. illa demens fugit in nemora fera;
ibi semper omne uitae spatium famula fuit.   90

Dea, magna Dea, Cybebe, Dea Domina
    Dindymi,
procul a mea tuos sit furor omnis, Era, domo.
alios age incitatos, alios age rabidos.

LXIV

Peliaco quondam prognatae uertice pinus
dicuntur liquidas Neptuni nasse per
    undas
Phasidos ad fluctus et fines Aeeteos,
cum lecti iuuenes, Argiuae robora pubis,
auratam optantes Colchis auertere pellem   5
ausi sunt uada salsa cita decurrere puppi,
caerula uerrentes abiegnis aequora palmis.
Diua quibus retinens in summis urbibus arces
ipsa leui fecit uolitantem flamine currum,
pinea coniungens inflexae texta carinae.   10
illa rudem cursu prora imbuit Amphitriten.
quae simul ac rostro uentosum proscidit aequor
tortaque remigio spumis incanuit unda,
emersere feri candenti e gurgite uultus,
aequoreae monstrum Nereides admirantes.   15
illa atque haud alia uiderunt luce marinas
mortales oculis nudato corpore Nymphas
nutricum tenus exstantes e gurgite cano.
tum Thetidis Peleus incensus fertur amore,
tum Thetis humanos non despexit hymenaeos,   20

Ferox, go toss the tawny mane on your muscular neck.'
So spake Cybébe, threatening, as her hand untied the
    yoke.
The beast, arousing himself, goaded his spirit to rage,   85
Rushed forward, roared, and trampled the brushwood
    with roving paw.
But when he approached the moist part of the whitening
    sea-shore
And saw there tender Attis beside the marbled deep,
He charges. She, demented, runs off to the wild woods;
There she remained at all times, life-long a female slave.   90

Goddess, great Goddess, Cybébe, Goddess Mistress of
    Dindymus,
Far from my house be all that frenzy of yours, O Queen.
Drive others to elation, drive others raving mad!

LXIV

Pines in the past, born from the brow of Pelion,
Are rumoured to have swum through Neptune's clear
    waves
To Phasis' breakers and the frontiers of Aeetes,
When chosen young men, oaks of Argive adulthood,
Eager to rob the Colchians of a gilded hide,   5
Ventured the voyage past salt shoals in a swift hull,
Sweeping blue-green levels with palms of silver fir.
For them the Goddess Guardian of high citadels
In person made a car to fly with the light breeze
By joining interwoven pinewood to curved keel.   10
Its prow inured raw Amphitrite to ships' courses.
As soon as with its beak it ploughed the windy plain
And, by oarage spiralled, wave grew white with foam,
Out of the gleaming surge wild faces arose,
Aequoreal Nereids, marvelling at the portent.   15
In that and not another day's light mortal eyes
Beheld the bodies of the Nymphs of Ocean naked
Far as the sucklers standing out from the white surge.
Then Peleus, it is told, for Thetis burned with love,
Then Thetis did not despise human hymeneals,   20

tum Thetidi Pater ipse iugandum Pelea
    sensit.
o nimis optato saeclorum tempore nati
heroes, saluete, Deum genus! o bona matrum
progenies saluete iter ⟨um mihi formosarum!⟩   23b
uos ego saepe, meo uos carmine compellabo,
teque adeo, eximie taedis felicibus aucte,   25
Thessaliae columen, Peleu, cui Iuppiter ipse,
ipse suos Diuum Genitor concessit amores.
tene Thetis tenuit pulccrrima Nereine?
tene suam Tethys concessit ducere neptem,
Oceanusque mari totum qui amplectitur orbem?   30

quae simul optatae finito tempore luces
aduenere, domum conuentu tota frequentat
Thessalia, oppletur laetanti regia coetu.
dona ferunt prae se, declarant gaudia uultu.
deseritur Cieros, linquunt Pthiotica Tempe   35
Crannonisque domos ac moenia Larisaea.
Pharsalum coeunt, Pharsalia tecta frequentant.
rura colit nemo, mollescunt colla iuuencis;
non humilis curuis purgatur uinea
    rastris;
non glebam prono conuellit uomere
    taurus;   40
non falx attenuat frondatorum arboris umbram;
squalida desertis rubigo infertur aratris.
ipsius at sedes, quacumque opulenta recessit
regia, fulgenti splendent auro atque
    argento.
candet ebur soliis, collucent pocula mensae,   45
tota domus gaudet regali splendida gaza.
puluinar uero Diuae geniale locatur
sedibus in mediis, Indo quod dente politum
tincta tegit roseo conchyli purpura fuco.

haec uestis priscis hominum uariata figuris   50
heroum mira uirtutes indicat arte.
namque fluentisono prospectans litore Diae,
Thesea cedentem celeri cum classe tuetur
indomitos in corde gerens Ariadna furores,

Then the Father Himself felt Peleus should yoke with
    Thetis.
O born in a time of all the ages too much missed,
Hail, heroes, breed of Gods! O noble progeny
Of mothers beautiful, I hail you once again!   23b
I shall invoke you often, invoke you in my song,
And you above all, blest by happy bridal torches,   25
Thessaly's pillar, Peleus, to whom Jove himself,
The Father of the Gods himself resigned his love.
Did Thetis, fairest Nereïne, embrace *you*?
Did Tethys allow *you* to wed her granddaughter
And Ocean's who encircles all the globe with sea?   30

But when at the appointed time those longed-for days
Arrived, the whole of Thessaly by invitation
Crowds the house, fills the palace with delighted throng.
They bring gifts with them. Faces manifest their joy.
Cieros is deserted; they leave Phthiotian Tempe   35
And Crannon's houses and the walls of Lárisa.
They flock to Pharsalus; they crowd Pharsalian roofs.
None tills the soil; the necks of oxen become soft.
No low-grown vine is cleared of weeds by bent-pronged
    rake.
No bullock cleaves the clod with deep-driven
    ploughshare.   40
No pruner's hook thins out the shade of leafy trees.
Slovenly rust attacks the solitary ploughs.
The king's own quarters, though, far as the sumptuous
Palace stretched backward, shine with lustrous gold and
    silver.
Ivory gleams on thrones, cups glow upon the board,   45
The whole house revels in the glint of royal treasure.
Indeed, there in the midst, the Goddess's bridal
Divan is placed, inlaid with Indian tooth and spread
With woven purple dipped in rosy murex dye.

This coverlet, embroidered with old-time human figures,   50
Reveals with wondrous art the virtues of heroes.
There, staring out from Dia's surf-resounding shore
And watching Theseus sailing off with his fast fleet,
Is Ariadne, nursing at heart unmastered passions,

necdum etiam sese quae uisit uisere credit,   55
utpote fallaci quae tum primum excita somno
desertam in sola miseram se cernat harena.
immemor at iuuenis fugiens pellit uada
    remis,
irrita uentosae linquens promissa procellae.
quem procul ex alga maestis Minois ocellis,   60
saxea ut effigies Bacchantis, prospicit, eheu,
prospicit et magnis curarum fluctuat undis,
non flauo retinens subtilem uertice mitram,
non contecta leui uelatum pectus amictu,
non tereti strophio lactentis uincta papillas,   65
omnia quae toto delapsa e corpore passim
ipsius ante pedes fluctus salis alludebant.
sed neque tum mitrae neque tum fluitantis amictus
illa uicem curans toto ex te pectore, Theseu,
toto animo, tota pendebat perdita mente.   70
a misera, assiduis quam luctibus externauit
spinosas Erycina serens in pectore curas
illa tempestate, ferox quo ex tempore Theseus
egressus curuis e litoribus Piraei
attigit iniusti regis Gortynia templa.   75

nam perhibent olim crudeli peste coactam
Androgeoneae poenas exsoluere caedis
electos iuuenes simul et decus innuptarum
Cecropiam solitam esse dapem dare Minotauro.
quis angusta malis cum moenia uexarentur,   80
ipse suum Theseus pro caris corpus Athenis
proicere optauit potius quam talia Cretam
funera Cecropiae nec-funera portarentur.
atque ita naue leui nitens ac lenibus auris
magnanimum ad Minoa uenit sedesque superbas.   85
hunc simul ac cupido conspexit lumine
    uirgo
regia, quam suauis exspirans castus odores
lectulus in molli complexu matris alebat,
quales Eurotae progignunt flumina myrtus
auraue distinctos educit uerna colores,   90

Nor can she yet believe she sees what she is seeing,   55
That very moment woken from deceiving sleep
To find her poor self left behind on lonely sand.
The heedless youth in flight strikes the shallows with
     oars,
Leaving broken promises to the blustering gale.
Him, far off, from the wrack Minois, bitter-eyed,   60
Like some Bacchante's stone statue, watches, ah
Watches, and tosses inwardly on great waves of troubles,
Not keeping fine-spun snood upon her golden head,
Not covered by light raiment over veiled bosom,
Not tied about the milky paps with rounded band,   65
All which had slipped down off her body in disarray
And at her feet salt waves were playing games with them.
But she, not thinking then of snood nor troubled then
By floating robe, with all her heart, Theseus, and all
Her soul and all her mind clung desperately to you.   70
Poor girl, how Erycina obsessed her with continual
Sorrows, sowing thorny worries in her heart
At that time, ever since the day when proud Theseus,
Sailing from the curving shoreline of Piraeus,
Touched land at the unjust king's Gortynian precinct.   75

For they report that earlier, forced by cruel plague
To pay the penalty for Androgeos' murder,
Cecropia used to send the pick of her young men
And glory of her maidens to feast the Minotaur.
But when her narrow walls were harossed by this evil,   80
Theseus of his own will determined to lay down
His body for dear Athens rather than allow
Cecropia's living dead thus to be shipped to Crete.
And so, relying on light vessel and fair winds,
He came to great-souled Minos and his proud abode.   85
Soon as the maiden princess with longing look espied
     him,
She whom a virgin bed breathing out sweet odours
Still nurtured in the soft embraces of her mother,
Like myrtle that the streams of Eurotas bring forth
Or like the different colours springtime air draws out,   90

non prius ex illo flagrantia declinauit
lumina quam cuncto concepit corpore
    flammam
funditus atque imis exarsit tota medullis.
heu, misere exagitans immiti corde furores,
Sancte Puer, curis hominum qui gaudia misces,   95
quaeque regis Golgos quaeque Idalium frondosum,
qualibus incensam iactastis mente puellam
fluctibus, in flauo saepe hospite suspirantem!
quantos illa tulit languenti corde timores!
quanto saepe magis fulgore expalluit auri,   100
cum saeuum cupiens contra contendere monstrum
aut mortem appeteret Theseus aut praemia laudis!
non ingrata tamen frustra munuscula Diuis
promittens tacito succendit uota labello.
nam uelut in summo quatientem bracchia Tauro   105
quercum aut conigeram sudanti cortice pinum
indomitus turbo contorquens flamine robur
eruit (illa procul radicitus exturbata
prona cadit, late quaeuiscumque obuia frangens),
sic domito saeuum prostrauit corpore Theseus   110
nequiquam uanis iactantem cornua uentis.
inde pedem sospes multa cum laude reflexit
errabunda regens tenui uestigia filo,
ne Labyrintheis e flexibus egredientem
tecti frustraretur inobseruabilis error.   115

sed quid ego a primo digressus carmine plura
commemorem, ut linquens genitoris filia uultum,
ut consanguineae complexum, ut denique matris
quae misera in gnata deperdita lamentatast,
omnibus his Thesei dulcem praeoptarit amorem;   120
aut ut uecta rati spumosa ad litora Diae
uenerit, aut ut eam deuinctam lumina somno
liquerit immemori discedens pectore coniunx?
saepe illam perhibent ardenti corde furentem
clarisonas imo fudisse e pectore
    uoces,   125
ac tum praeruptos tristem conscendere
    montes

She did not turn away from him her smouldering
Eye-beams until throughout her frame she had caught
    fire
Deep down, and in her inmost marrow was all ablaze.
Ah, wretchedly arousing passions, cruel-hearted,
Holy Child, who mix for mankind joy with sorrow,   95
And you, the Queen of Golgi and leafy Idalium,
On what rough seas you tossed the girl with mind aflame
As often as she sighed for that fair-haired stranger!
How great the fears she suffered with a heavy heart!
How often then she turned paler than gleam of gold,   100
When, eager to contend against the savage monster,
Theseus willed either death or the prize of glory!
Not vainly pledging, though, to the Gods unpleasing
Little gifts she kindled vows on silent lips.
For as on Taurus' top, wildly waving its arms,   105
Oaktree or cone-bearing pine with sticky bark
By a furious whirlwind whose blast twists its stout trunk
Is toppled (torn up by the roots the tree full length
Falls prostrate, crushing everything in its wide way),
So Theseus laid the monster low, beast body beaten   110
As it tossed its useless horns against the empty air.
Thence with great renown he walked his way back, safe,
Directing his bewildered steps with slender thread,
Lest, while he tried to escape the Labyrinth's meanders,
The building's inscrutable maze should baffle him.   115

But why digressing further from my opening song
Remember how the daughter leaving her sire's face,
Leaving the embrace of blood-sister and even of mother
Who grieved in desperation for her wretched child,
Before all these preferred the sweet love of Theseus?   120
Or how he carried her by ship to Dia's foaming
Beaches, or how he left her blindfolded by sleep,
Departing, though her husband, with a heedless heart?
Often, they say, in frenzy, with her mind on fire,
She poured out shrill-edged cries from the depth of her
    heart,   125
And sometimes in her sorrow she clambered up steep
    cliffs

unde aciem in pelagi uastos protenderet
   aestus,
tum tremuli salis aduersas procurrere in undas
mollia nudatae tollentem tegmina surae,
atque haec extremis maestam dixisse querellis,   130
frigidulos udo singultus ore cientem:
'sicine me patriis auectam, perfide, ab aris,
perfide, deserto liquisti in litore, Theseu?
sicine discedens, neglecto numine Diuum,
immemor, a, deuota domum periuria portas?   135
nullane res potuit crudelis flectere mentis
consilium? tibi nulla fuit clementia praesto,
immite ut nostri uellet miserescere pectus?
at non haec quondam blanda promissa dedisti
uoce mihi, non haec miseram sperare iubebas,   140
sed conubia laeta, sed optatos hymenaeos,
quae cuncta aerii discerpunt irrita uenti.
nunc iam nulla uiro iuranti femina credat,
nulla uiri speret sermones esse fideles;
quis dum aliquid cupiens animus praegestit apisci,   145
nil metuunt iurare, nihil promittere
   parcunt,
sed simul ac cupidae mentis satiata libido est,
dicta nihil meminere, nihil periuria curant.
certe ego te in medio uersantem turbine
   leti
eripui, et potius germanum amittere creui   150
quam tibi fallaci supremo in tempore dessem.
pro quo dilaceranda feris dabor alitibusque
praeda, neque iniacta tumulabor mortua terra.
quaenam te genuit sola sub rupe leaena,
quod mare conceptum spumantibus exspuit
   undis,   155
quae Syrtis, quae Scylla rapax, quae uasta
   Charybdis,
talia qui reddis pro dulci praemia uita?
si tibi non cordi fuerant conubia nostra,
saeua quod horrebas prisci praecepta
   parentis,
attamen in uestras potuisti ducere sedes   160

From whence to extend her view of the ocean's empty
    swell;
Sometimes ran out to meet the restless brine's breakers
Kilting up her bared legs' lightweight covering.
These words at last she spoke of bitter lamentation,   130
Distorting with chill little sobs her tearful face:
'So, faithless one who took me from my father's altars,
You leave me, faithless Theseus, on a lonely beach?
So, sailing off, contemptuous of the Gods' will,
You carry home, ah heedless, accursed perjury?   135
And was there nothing that could turn your cruel mind's
Intention? Had you then no kindliness at call
That your ungentle heart might wish to pity us?
Not these the promises you gave me once in gallant
Phrases, not these the things you told poor me to expect,   140
But married happiness, but longed-for hymeneals,
All which the airy winds have tattered into nothing.
No woman now should put her faith in a man's oath
And none expect a man's word to be trustworthy.
For while their lusting spirit craves to gain something   145
There's nothing they fear to swear, nothing forbear to
    promise;
But once the longing of their lustful mind is slaked
They don't recall their words or balk at perjury.
You can't deny that while you spun round in death's
    whirlpool
I rescued you and chose rather to lose a brother   150
Than fail deceitful you in time of utmost need—
For which I'm to be torn apart by beasts and birds,
Carrion in death, with no dust thrown for burial.
What lioness littered you below some lonely crag?
What sea conceived and spewed you out in the waves'
    spume?   155
What Syrtis, what devouring Scylla, what grim
    Charybdis,
You who can render such return for your sweet life?
If marriage, yours and mine, had not been to your mind
Because you dreaded the harsh rules of an old-world
    father,
You could at least have brought me to your family home   160

quae tibi iucundo famularer serua labore,
candida permulcens liquidis uestigia lymphis,
purpureaue tuum consternens ueste cubile.
sed quid ego ignaris nequiquam conqueror auris,
externata malo, quae nullis sensibus auctae   165
nec missas audire queunt nec reddere uoces?
ille autem prope iam mediis uersatur in undis,
nec quisquam apparet uacua mortalis in alga.
sic, nimis insultans extremo tempore, saeua
Fors etiam nostris inuidit questibus aures.   170
Iuppiter Omnipotens, utinam ne tempore primo
Cnosia Cecropiae tetigissent litora puppes,
indomito nec dira ferens stipendia tauro
perfidus in Creta religasset nauita funem,
nec malus hic celans dulci crudelia forma   175
consilia in nostris requiesset sedibus hospes!
nam quo me referam? quali spe perdita nitor?
Idaeosne petam montes? a, gurgite lato
discernens ponti truculentum ubi diuidit aequor?
an patris auxilium sperem? quemne ipsa reliqui   180
respersum iuuenem fraterna caede secuta?
coniugis an fido consoler memet amore?
quine fugit lentos incuruans gurgite remos?
praeterea nullo colitur sola insula tecto,
nec patet egressus pelagi cingentibus undis.   185
nulla fugae ratio, nulla spes. omnia muta,
omnia sunt deserta, ostentant omnia letum.
non tamen ante mihi languescent lumina morte
nec prius a fesso secedent corpore sensus
quam iustam a Diuis exposcam prodita multam   190
Caelestumque fidem postrema comprecer hora.
quare facta uirum multantes uindice
      poena
Eumenides, quibus anguino redimita capillo
frons exspirantis praeportat pectoris
      iras,
huc huc aduentate, meas audite querellas,   195
quas ego, uae misera, extremis proferre
      medullis
cogor inops, ardens, amenti caeca furore.

That I might serve you as a slave in joyful work,
Soothing the white soles of your feet in clear water
Or spreading your couch with a purple coverlet.
But why do I complain, out of my mind with woe,
In vain to unheeding airs, which unpossessed of feeling   165
Can neither hear nor return a spoken message?
Besides, by now he's almost half way on the waves
And there's no sign of man along the bare sea-wrack.
So, jumping on us hard in time's extremity,
Cruel Fortune even grudges ears to our complaints.   170
Almighty Jove, if only in that first of times
Cecropian hulls had never touched the Cnossian shore,
Nor bearing fearful tribute to an untamed bull
Had faithless sailor ever tied up line in Crete
Or this bad man, concealing cruel counsels under   175
A sweet outside had rested in our house as guest!
For where do I turn? What hope rely on in my ruin?
Am I to make for Ida's mountains? Ah, with wide
Gulf sundering, when stormy ocean lies between?
Or can I hope for father's help? Whom I deserted   180
To follow a youth spattered with my brother's blood?
Or comfort myself with a husband's faithful love?
Who's fleeing from me, bending tough oars in the surge?
Besides, this lonely island's uninhabited.
Every way out is blocked by sea's encircling waves.   185
There's no means of escape, no hope. Everything's dumb,
Everywhere's deserted, everything threatens doom.
Nevertheless my eyes shall not grow dim in death
Neither shall sensation leave my weary body
Before I claim, betrayed, just forfeit from the Gods   190
And pray in my last hour for Heaven to keep faith.
Wherefore, chastisers of men's deeds with vengeful
       forfeit,
Eumenides, whose forehead wreathed in snaky hair
Proclaims the furious anger breathed out from your
       heart,
Be present, come in haste, give ear to my complaints,   195
Which, woe is me, I am forced to bring forth from my
       very
Marrow, helpless, burning, blinded by mindless passion.

quae quoniam uerae nascuntur pectore ab imo,
uos nolite pati nostrum uanescere luctum,
sed quali solam Theseus me mente reliquit,   200
tali mente, Deae, funestet seque
   suosque.'

has postquam maesto profudit pectore
   uoces,
supplicium saeuis exposcens anxia factis,
annuit inuicto Caelestum numine Rector;
quo motu tellus atque horrida contremuerunt   205
aequora concussitque micantia sidera mundus.
ipse autem caeca mentem caligine
   Theseus
consitus oblito dimisit pectore cuncta
quae mandata prius constanti mente tenebat,
dulcia nec maesto sustollens signa parenti   210
sospitem Erectheum se ostendit uisere portum.
namque ferunt olim, classi cum moenia Diuae
linquentem gnatum uentis concrederet Aegeus,
talia complexum iuueni mandata
   dedisse:
'gnate mihi longa iucundior unice uita,   215
gnate ego quem in dubios cogor dimittere casus,
reddite in extrema nuper mihi fine senectae,
quandoquidem fortuna mea ac tua feruida uirtus
eripit inuito mihi te, cui languida nondum
lumina sunt gnati cara saturata figura,   220
non ego te gaudens laetanti pectore mittam
nec te ferre sinam fortunae signa secundae,
sed primum multas expromam mente querellas,
canitiem terra atque infuso puluere foedans,
inde infecta uago suspendam lintea malo,   225
nostros ut luctus nostraeque incendia mentis
carbasus obscurata dicet ferrugine Hibera.
quod tibi si sancti concesserit Incola Itoni,
quae nostrum genus ac sedes defendere Erecthei
annuit, ut tauri respergas sanguine
   dextram,   230
tum uero facito ut memori tibi condita
   corde

But since they are true children of my inmost heart
Be sure you suffer not our grief to go for nothing,
But with what mind Theseus has left me on my own,   200
With such mind, Goddesses, let him doom himself and
   his.'

After she had poured forth these words from her sad
   heart,
In anguish claiming punishment for cruel deeds,
Heaven's Ruler nodded his invincible assent,
And at that movement earth and the wild sea's expanse   205
Quaked and the firmament shook its glittering stars.
But Theseus' self, his mind thick-sown with blinding
   dark,
Let slip from his forgetful heart all the commands
Which hitherto he had kept constantly in mind,
Nor hoisted the sweet signal for his grieving parent   210
To prove that he was safely in sight of Erechtheus' port.
For earlier, we are told, commending to the winds
The son about to sail from the Goddess's walls,
Aegeus embraced the youth and gave him these
   commands:
'My only son, sweeter than length of life to me,   215
Son I am forced to send away to doubtful doom,
Though late restored to me in my extreme old age,
Whereas my fortune and your passionate valour
Rob me of you against my will (for my dim eyes
Have not yet looked their fill upon my son's dear form)   220
I shall not send you gladly with a happy heart
Nor let you show the signs of favourable fortune
But first give utterance to my mind's much bitterness
Befouling my white hair with soil and sprinkled dust,
Thereafter hang the roving mast with dyed canvas   225
So that the grief and burning kindled in our mind
Sails darkened with Iberian rust may publicize.
But should the Dweller in holy Itonus give you leave
(She who vouchsafes protection to our people and
Erechtheus' realm) to stain your right hand with bull's
   blood,   230
Then, truly, see that these commands stay fresh, stored
   up

haec uigeant mandata nec ulla oblitteret aetas,
ut simul ac nostros inuisent lumina collis,
funestam antennae deponant undique uestem
candidaque intorti sustollant uela rudentes,   235
quam primum cernens ut laeta gaudia mente
agnoscam, cum te reducem aetas prospera
     sistet.'
haec mandata prius constanti mente tenentem
Thesea ceu pulsae uentorum flamine nubes
aerium niuci montis liquere cacumen.   240
at pater, ut summa prospectum ex arce petebat,
anxia in assiduos absumens lumina fletus,
cum primum inflati conspexit lintea ueli,
praecipitem scse scopulorum e uertice
     iecit,
amissum credens immiti Thesea fato.   245
sic, funesta domus ingressus tecta paterna
morte, ferox Theseus, qualem Minoidi luctum
obtulerat mente immemori, talem ipse recepit.
quae tum prospectans cedentem maesta carinam
multiplices animo uoluebat saucia curas.   250

at parte ex alia florens uolitabat Iacchus
cum thiaso Satyrorum et Nysigenis Silenis,
te quaerens, Ariadna, tuoque incensus amore.
cui Thyades passim lymphata mente furebant
'euhoe' bacchantes 'euhoe', capita inflectentes.   255
harum pars tecta quatiebant cuspide thyrsos,
pars e diuolso iactabant membra iuuenco,
pars sese tortis serpentibus
     incingebant,
pars obscura cauis celebrabant orgia cistis,
orgia quae frustra cupiunt audire profani.   260
plangebant aliae proceris tympana palmis
aut tereti tenuis tinnitus aere ciebant.
multis raucisonos efflabant cornua bombos
barbaraque horribili stridebat tibia cantu.

talibus amplifice uestis decorata figuris   265
puluinar complexa suo uelabat amictu.
quae postquam cupide spectando Thessala pubes
expleta est, sanctis coepit decedere Diuis.

In mindful heart and unerased by lapse of time,
That when your bright eyes first catch sight of our hills
The yard-arms lower their doom-laden cloth entirely
And plaited halyards hoist aloft shining white sails,   235
That seeing I may know your joy with happy mind
Soon as may be, when prospering time brings you back
        safe.'
These commands, hitherto kept constantly in mind,
Drifted from Theseus like clouds driven by the wind's
Breath from the airy summit of a snowy mountain.   240
His father, though, on look-out from the Acropolis
And wasting anguished eyes in continual weeping,
Soon as he saw the canvas of the swelling sail
Hurled himself headlong down from the highest of the
        rocks,
Believing Theseus lost to an ungentle fate.   245
So, entering the home polluted by his father's
Death, haughty Theseus had himself to endure such grief
As he had brought Minois by his heedless mind,
Who meanwhile, sadly watching his receding keel,
Wounded in spirit pondered troubles manifold.   250

But in another part Iacchus in bloom flew by
With rout of Satyrs and Nysigenous Sileni,
Seeking you, Ariadne, and burning with love for you.
For him the Thyads raved around with frenzied mind,
Shrieking *Evoe, Evoe*, twisting their heads about.   255
Part of them were shaking *thyrsi* with covered spike,
Part threw around the limbs of a dismembered steer,
Part wrapped themselves about with wreaths of writhing
        snakes,
Part thronged the *orgia* concealed in hollow creels,
Those *orgia* the profane desire in vain to hear.   260
Others with open palms were banging tambourines
Or clashing ringing clangour from thin rounded bronze.
For many, horns blared out cacophonous *boom-booms*
And barbarous reed-pipes screeched hair-raising music.

The coverlet, with such figures grandly decorated,   265
Embracing the divan veiled and enveloped it;
With eager study of which after Thessaly's folk
Were sated, they made way then for the holy Gods.

hic, qualis flatu placidum mare matutino
horrificans Zephyrus procliuas incitat undas 270
(Aurora exoriente uagi sub limina
   Solis)
quae tarde primum clementi flamine pulsae
procedunt leuiterque sonant plangore cachinni,
post uento crescente magis magis increbrescunt
purpureaque procul nantes ab luce refulgent, 275
sic tum uestibulo linquentes regia tecta
ad se quisque uago passim pede discedebant.
quorum post abitum princeps e uertice Peli
aduenit Chiron portans siluestria dona.
nam quoscumque ferunt campi, quos Thessala magnis 280
montibus ora creat, quos propter fluminis
   undas
aura parit flores tepidi fecunda Fauoni,
hos indistinctis plexos tulit ipse
   corollis,
quo permulsa domus iucundo risit
   odore.
confestim Penios adest, uiridantia Tempe, 285
Tempe quae siluae cingunt super impendentes,
Haemonisin linquens Dryasin celebranda choreis,
non uacuos; namque ille tulit radicitus altas
fagos ac recto proceras stipite laurus
non sine nutanti platano lentaque sorore 290
flammati Phaëthontis et aeria cupressu.
haec circum sedes late contexta locauit
uestibulum ut molli uelatum fronde
   uireret.
post hunc consequitur sollerti corde Prometheus,
extenuata gerens ueteris uestigia poenae 295
quam quondam silici restrictus membra catena
persoluit pendens e uerticibus praeruptis.
inde Pater Diuum sancta cum coniuge natisque
aduenit caelo, te solum, Phoebe, relinquens
unigenamque simul cultricem montibus Idri; 300
Pelea nam tecum pariter soror aspernata est
nec Thetidis taedas uoluit celebrare iugalis.

Here, even as Zephyrus ruffling the tranquil sea
With early morning breath arouses the slope waves   270
(While Dawn comes up to the threshold of the roving
      Sun)
Which slowly at first, being driven by a clement breeze,
Procéss and lightly break with a mournful guffaw,
Then, the wind strengthening, grow bigger, multiply
And swimming in the distance gleam with crimson light,   275
So, by the forecourt then leaving the royal palace,
The guests dispersed on roving feet each to his home.
And after their departure, first of all, from Pelion's
Summit Chiron came, bringing woodland gifts.
For all the flowers the plains bear, all that Thessaly   280
Grows on her mighty mountains, all that warm
      Favonius'
Fruitful breeze produces near the rippling river,
All these he brought himself, arranged in random
      bunches,
Charmed by whose delightful fragrance the house
      laughed.
Straightway Peníos comes, leaving verdant Tempe,   285
Tempe by overhanging woodland ringed above,
For the Haemonian Dryads to celebrate with dances,
Not empty-handed, for he carried, root and all,
Lofty beeches and tall laurels with straight stem,
Not without nodding plane-trees and the supple sister   290
Of burnt-out Phaëthon and airy cypresses.
These he placed all around the entrance, intertwined,
So that the forecourt might grow green, screened with
      soft leaves.
There follows after him Promethcus of crafty heart,
Bearing faded traces of the ancient punishment   295
Which formerly, with limbs fast bound by chain to flint,
He paid by hanging over a sheer precipice.
Then the Father of Gods with holy wife and children
Arrived from Heaven, leaving you, Phoebus, alone
Together with the sibling Dweller on Idrus' mountains;   300
For equally with you your sister despised Peleus
And refused to attend Thetis' nuptial torches.

qui postquam niueis flexerunt sedibus artus,
large multiplici constructae sunt dape mensae,
cum interea infirmo quatientes corpora motu   305
ueridicos Parcae coeperunt edere cantus.
his corpus tremulum complectens undique uestis
candida purpurea talos incinxerat ora,
at roseae niueo residebant uertice uittae,
aeternumque manus carpebant rite laborem.   310
laeua colum molli lana retinebat amictum;
dextera tum leuiter deducens fila
  supinis
formabat digitis, tum prono in pollice
  torquens
libratum tereti uersabat turbine fusum;
atque ita decerpens aequabat semper opus
  dens,   315
laneaque aridulis haerebant morsa labellis
quae prius in leui fuerant exstantia filo.
ante pedes autem candentis mollia lanae
uellera uirgati custodibant calathisci.
haec tum clarisona uellentes uellera
  uoce   320
talia diuino fuderunt carmine fata,
carmine perfidiae quod post nulla arguet aetas.

'o decus eximium magnis uirtutibus augens,
Emathiae tutamen, Opis carissime nato,
accipe quod laeta tibi pandunt luce Sorores,   325
ueridicum oraclum. sed uos, quae fata sequuntur
 currite ducentes subtegmina, currite, fusi.

adueniet tibi iam portans optata
  maritis
Hesperus, adueniet fausto cum sidere coniunx
quae tibi flexanimo mentem perfundat amore   330
languidulosque paret tecum coniungere somnos,
leuia substernens robusto bracchia collo.
 currite ducentes subtegmina, currite, fusi.

nulla domus tales umquam contexit amores,
nullus amor tali coniunxit foedere amantes   335
qualis adest Thetidi, qualis concordia Peleo.
 currite ducentes subtegmina, currite, fusi.

But after they had bent their limbs to snow-white seats,
The tables were heaped lavishly with various courses;
Meanwhile, their bodies shaking with infirmity, 305
The three Parcae began to chant their soothsaying.
A fair white robe embracing all their trembling body
Fell about their ankles with its purple edge,
While rosy fillets rested on their snow-white heads
And their hands duly plied the everlasting task. 310
The left hand held the distaff mantled in soft wool;
The right, first, lightly drawing down the threads with
    upturned
Fingers shaped them, then, with downturned thumb
    twisting,
Revolved the spindle balanced by its rounded whorl;
And all the time their teeth tore off and smoothed the
    work 315
And to their thin dry lips clung bitten tufts of wool
Which previously obtruded on the even thread.
Moreover at their feet the soft fleeces of dazzling
White wool were safely stored in plaited osier baskets.
They then, plucking the fleeces, with clear-sounding
    voice 320
Poured out in a prophetic song such fates as these—
A song no after-age will ever charge with falsehood:

'O you, enhancing rare distinction with great virtues,
Emathia's guardian, most dear to the son of Ops,
Hear what the sisters scry for you in this glad light, 325
Their truthful oracle. But you that the fates follow
    Run, spindles, drawing out the weft, run on.

For you there'll come soon, bringing heart's desire to
    bridegrooms,
Hesperus; with his lucky star there'll come a consort
To bathe your being for you in soul-searching love 330
And ready to consort with you in swooning slumbers,
Laying her smooth arms underneath your stalwart neck.
    Run, spindles, drawing out the weft, run on.

No house has ever given shelter to such loves,
No love has ever joined lovers in such treaty 335
As is the harmony between Peleus and Thetis.
    Run, spindles, drawing out the weft, run on.

nascetur uobis expers terroris Achilles,
hostibus haud tergo sed forti pectore notus,
qui persaepe uago uictor certamine cursus   340
flammea praeuertet celeris uestigia ceruae.
    currite ducentes subtegmina, currite, fusi.

non illi quisquam bello se conferet heros
cum Phrygii Teucro manabunt sanguine campi,
Troicaque obsidens longinquo moenia bello   345
periuri Pelopis uastabit tertius heres.
    currite ducentes subtegmina, currite, fusi.

illius egregias uirtutes claraque facta
saepe fatebuntur gnatorum in funere matres,
cum incultum cano soluent a uertice
    crinem   350
putriaque infirmis uariabunt pectora
    palmis.
    currite ducentes subtegmina, currite, fusi.

namque uelut densas praecerpens messor aristas
sole sub ardenti flauentia demetit arua,
Troiugenum infesto prosternet corpora
    ferro.   355
    currite ducentes subtegmina, currite, fusi.

testis erit magnis uirtutibus unda Scamandri,
quae passim rapido diffunditur Hellesponto,
cuius iter caesis angustans corporum
    aceruis
alta tepefaciet permixta flumina caede.   360
    currite ducentes subtegmina, currite, fusi.

denique testis erit morti quoque reddita praeda
cum teres excelso coaceruatum aggere bustum
excipiet niueos perculsae uirginis
    artus.
    currite ducentes subtegmina, currite, fusi.   365

nam simul ac fessis dederit Fors copiam Achiuis
urbis Dardaniae Neptunia soluere uincla,
alta Polyxenia madefient caede sepulcra;
quae, uelut ancipiti succumbens uictima ferro,
proiciet truncum summisso poplite corpus.   370
    currite ducentes subtegmina, currite, fusi.

There shall be born to you one free from fear—Achilles,
Known to the enemy not by back but valiant front,
Who many a time victorious in far-ranging race   340
Will overtake the fiery slots of the swift deer.
    Run, spindles, drawing out the weft, run on.

There's not a hero shall compare with him in war,
When plains of Phrygia shall flow with Teucrian blood
And in the siege of that long war the walls of Troy   345
Shall be destroyed by the third heir of perjured Pelops.
    Run, spindles, drawing out the weft, run on.

His extraordinary virtues and famed deeds
Shall mothers often own at their sons' funeral,
When they shall loose dishevelled hair from their white
    crowns   350
And with impotent palms shall bruise their withered
    breasts.
    Run, spindles, drawing out the weft, run on.

For as a reaper lopping off the close-packed corn-ears
Beneath the burning sun reaps golden-yellow ploughland,
He shall cut down with raised steel bodies of Trojan-
    born.   355
    Run, spindles, drawing out the weft, run on.

Scamander's wave shall witness to his great virtues,
Which spreads out every way in the swift Hellespont
And whose course he will choke with slaughtered heaps
    of bodies,
Warming the deep river with intermingled blood.   360
    Run, spindles, drawing out the weft, run on.

Last witness will be the prize given him even in death
When heaped up in a lofty mound his rounded tomb
Duly receives the snow-white limbs of a butchered
    virgin.
    Run, spindles, drawing out the weft, run on.   365

For soon as Fortune grants the weary Achaeans means
To undo Neptune's knot around the Dardan city,
His high tomb will be drenched in Polyxena's blood,
Who, like a slain beast falling to the two-edged sword,
Shall lay down, sinking to her knees, a headless body.   370
    Run, spindles, drawing out the weft, run on.

quare agite, optatos animi coniungite amores.
accipiat coniunx felici foedere Diuam,
dedatur cupido iamdudum nupta marito.
   currite ducentes subtegmina, currite, fusi.   375

non illam nutrix orienti luce reuisens
hesterno collum poterit circumdare filo,   377
anxia nec mater discordis maesta
    puellae   379
secubitu caros mittet sperare nepotes.   380
   currite ducentes subtegmina, currite, fusi.'

talia praefantes quondam felicia Pelei
carmina diuino cecinerunt pectore Parcae.
praesentes namque ante domos inuisere castas
heroum et sese mortali ostendere
    coetu   385
Caelicolae nondum spreta pietate solebant.
saepe Pater Diuum templo in fulgente residens
annua cum festis uenissent sacra diebus,
conspexit terra centum procumbere
    tauros.
saepe uagus Liber Parnasi uertice summo   390
Thyiadas effusis euantis crinibus egit,
cum Delphi tota certatim ex urbe ruentes
acciperent laeti Diuum fumantibus aris.
saepe in letifero belli certamine Mauors
aut rapidi Tritonis Era aut Amarynthia Virgo   395
armatas hominum est praesens hortata
    cateruas.
sed postquam Tellus scelere est imbuta nefando
iustitiamque omnes cupida de mente fugarunt,
perfudere manus fraterno sanguine fratres,
destitit extinctos gnatus lugere parentes,   400
optauit genitor primaeui funera nati
liber uti nuptae poteretur flore nouellae,
ignaro mater substernens se impia nato,
impia non uerita est diuos scelerare Penates.
omnia fanda nefanda malo permixta furore   405
iustificam nobis mentem auertere Deorum.
quare nec talis dignantur uisere coetus
nec se contingi patiuntur lumine claro.

Come therefore and consort in long-imagined love.
Her consort shall accept the Goddess in glad treaty
And at long last shall bride be given to eager groom.
   Run spindles, drawing out the weft, run on.   375

Her nurse revisiting her at first light tomorrow
Shall fail to tie yesterday's ribbon round her neck,   377
Nor shall an anxious mother, sad at her quarrelling
    daughter   379
Sleeping apart, stop hoping for dear grandchildren.   380
   Run, spindles, drawing out the weft, run on.'

Foretelling in the past such happiness for Peleus
From their inspired breast the Parcae sang their song.
For long ago Heaven's Dwellers in person used to visit
The chaste homes of heroes and show themselves at
    mortal   385
Meetings, while religion was not yet held in scorn.
Often the Father of Gods, enthroned in shining temple,
When with their festal days his annual rites had come,
Would watch one hundred bulls slump prostrate to the
    ground.
Often nomadic Liber from Parnassus' top   390
Would drive his baying Thyads with their hair flying,
While Delphians in concert rushing from their town
Gave the God joyous welcome with smoke of sacrifice.
And often Mavors in war's deadly competition
Or rapid Triton's Lady or the Amarynthian Maid   395
Would hearten by their presence armed companies of
    men.
But after Earth was stained with crime unspeakable
And all evicted Justice from their greedy thoughts,
Brothers poured the blood of brothers on their hands,
Sons no longer grieved when parents passed away,   400
Father prayed for death of son in his first youth
So as freely to possess the bloom of a new bride,
Mother, lying impiously with ignorant son,
Dared impiously to sin against divine Penates.
Our evil madness by confounding fair with foul   405
Has turned away from us the Gods' forgiving thoughts.
Wherefore they neither deign to visit such meetings
Nor let themselves be touched by light of day or eye.

LXV

Etsi me assiduo confectum cura dolore
    seuocat a Doctis, Hortale, Virginibus,
nec potis est dulcis Musarum expromere
      fetus
    mens animi, tantis fluctuat ipsa malis—
namque mei nuper Lethaeo gurgite fratris   5
    pallidulum manans alluit unda pedem,
Troia Rhoeteo quem subter litore tellus
    ereptum nostris obterit ex oculis.
⟨numquam ego te potero posthac audire loquentem?⟩
    numquam ego te, uita frater amabilior,   10
aspiciam posthac? at certe semper amabo,
    semper maesta tua carmina morte canam,
qualia sub densis ramorum concinit
      umbris
    Daulias absumpti fata gemens Ityli—
sed tamen in tantis maeroribus, Hortale, mitto   15
    haec expressa tibi carmina Battiadae,
ne tua dicta uagis nequiquam credita
      uentis
    effluxisse meo forte putes animo,
ut missum sponsi furtiuo munere malum
    procurrit casto uirginis e gremio,   20
quod miserae oblitae molli sub ueste locatum,
    dum aduentu matris prosilit, excutitur,
atque illud prono praeceps agitur decursu,
    huic manat tristi conscius ore rubor.

LXVI

Omnia qui magni dispexit lumina mundi,
    qui stellarum ortus comperit atque obitus,
flammeus ut rapidi solis nitor obscuretur,
    ut cedant certis sidera temporibus,
ut Triuiam furtim sub Latmia saxa relegans   5
    dulcis amor gyro deuocet aerio,
idem me ille Conon caelesti in limine uidit
    e Beroniceo uertice caesariem

LXV

Though I am worn out with long grieving, Hortalus,
  And care recalls me from the Learnèd Maids,
Nor can my mind's thought bring forth sweet births of
    the Muses,
  Being tossed itself on a tide of troubles—
For lately a wave rising on the flood of Lethe   5
  Lapped the pale foot of my poor brother,
Whom the land of Troy has snatched away from our sight
  And crushes beneath the Rhoetéan shore.
⟨Shall I never again be able to hear you speaking?⟩
  Shall I never, brother more lovable than life,   10
Set eyes on you again? But surely I shall always love you,
  Always sing songs saddened by your death,
Like those the Daulian sings beneath the boughs' thick
    shade
  As she mourns the fate of murdered Itylus—
Yet still despite such sorrows, Hortalus, I send   15
  These songs of Battiades translated for you,
Lest maybe you should think your words were vainly
    spent
  On the wandering winds and slipped my mind,
As when an apple, sent as a clandestine gift
  By her fiancé, rolls down from a girl's chaste lap;   20
Stowed in her soft dress by the poor forgetful thing,
  When she jumps up on mother's entry it is shaken out
And tumbles down, bumping forward along the floor;
  A guilty blush rises on her rueful face.

LXVI

He who distinguished all the lights in the firmament,
  Who learnt the risings and settings of stars,
How the devouring Sun's fiery sheen is darkened,
  How constellations fade out at fixed times,
How secretly banishing Diana to rocky Latmos   5
  Sweet love calls her down from her airy round,
That same Conon saw me in the floor of heaven,
  The lock of hair from Berenice's head,

fulgentem clare, quam cunctis illa Deorum
  leuia protendens bracchia pollicita est,   10
qua rex tempestate nouo auctus hymenaeo
  uastatum finis iuerat Assyrios,
dulcia nocturnae portans uestigia rixae
  quam de uirgineis gesserat exuuiis.
estne nouis nuptis odio Venus? anne parentum   15
  frustrantur falsis gaudia lacrimulis
ubertim thalami quas intra limina fundunt?
  non, ita me Diui, uera gcmunt, iuerint.
id mea me multis docuit regina querellis
  inuisente nouo proelia torua uiro.   20
an tu non orbum luxti deserta cubile
  sed fratris cari flebile discidium?
quam penitus maestas exedit cura medullas!
  ut tibi tunc toto pectore sollicitae
sensibus ereptis mens excidit! at te ego certe   25
  cognoram a parua uirgine magnanimam.
anne bonum oblita es facinus quo regium adepta es
  coniugium, quod non fortior ausit alis?
sed tum maesta uirum mittens quae uerba locuta
    es!
  Iuppiter, ut tersti lumina saepe manu!   · 30
quis te mutauit tantus Deus? an quod
    amantes
  non longe a caro corpore abesse uolunt?
atque ibi me cunctis pro dulci coniuge
    Diuis
  non sine taurino sanguine pollicita es,
si reditum tetulisset. is haut in tempore longo   35
  captam Asiam Aegypti finibus addiderat.
quis ego pro factis caelesti reddita coetu
  pristina uota nouo munere dissoluo.
inuita, o regina, tuo de uertice cessi,
  inuita, adiuro teque tuumque caput,   40
digna ferat quod siquis inaniter adiurarit.
  sed qui se ferro postulet esse parem?
ille quoque euersus mons est quem maximum in
    oris
  progenies Thiae clara superuehitur,

Shining brightly, which she promised to all of the Gods,
   Stretching out smooth arms in prayer,   10
What time the king, increased by his new hymeneals,
   Had gone to ravage Assyrian borders,
Bearing sweet traces of the nocturnal struggle
   He had ventured on for a virgin prize.
Do new brides indeed hate Venus? Or do they spoil   15
   The joy of parents with deceitful tears
Shed abundantly inside the marriage chamber?
   So help me Gods, their grief is false.
I learnt this from my Queen's many lamentations
   While her new man directed grim battles.   20
Or did you grieve, abandoned, not for widowed bed
   but for sad parting from dear brother?
How deeply concern ate into your mournful marrow!
   How with all your heart you worried then,
Robbed of your senses, bereft of reason! Yet sure I knew   25
   That even as a little girl you were high-spirited.
Have you forgotten that good deed which won for you
   A royal marriage, deed no stronger would have dared?
But what sad words you spoke then, bidding your man
     goodbye!
   Jupiter, how often your hand dried your eyes!   30
What great God altered you? Or was it because lovers
     wish
   Not to be far away from the belovèd body?
And it was then you vowed me, not without blood of
     bulls,
   To all the Gods for your sweet husband's sake
Should he make safe return. In no long time he added   35
   Conquered Asia to Egypt's borders,
For which achievement I discharge the past vow
   As a present gift paid to heaven's host.
Unwillingly, O Queen, I parted from your brow,
   Unwillingly, I swear by you and your head,   40
By which if any lightly swear let him get his deserts.
   But who can claim to be a match for iron?
Even that mountain was thrown down, the region's
     greatest,
   Which Thia's brilliant offspring traverses,

cum Medi peperere nouum mare cumque iuuentus   45
  per medium classi barbara nauit Athon.
quid facient crines cum ferro talia
    cedant?
  Iuppiter, ut Chalybon omne genus pereat,
et qui principio sub terra quaerere
    uenas
  institit ac ferri stringere duritiem!   50
abiunctae paulo ante comae mea fata sorores
  lugebant cum se Memnonis Aethiopis
unigena, impellens nutantibus aera pennis,
  obtulit, Arsinoes Locridos ales equos,
isque per aetherias me tollens auolat umbras   55
  et Veneris casto collocat in gremio.
ipsa suum Zephyritis eo famulum legarat,
  Graiia Canopitis incola litoribus.
hic liquidi uario ne solum in limine caeli
  ex Ariadneis aurea temporibus   60
fixa corona foret, sed nos quoque fulgeremus
  deuotae flaui uerticis exuuiae,
uuidulam a fletu cedentem ad templa Deum
    me
  sidus in antiquis Diua nouum posuit.
Virginis et saeui contingens namque Leonis   65
  lumina, Callisto iuncta Lycaoniae,
uertor in occasum, tardum dux ante Booten,
  qui uix sero alto mergitur Oceano.
sed quamquam me nocte premunt uestigia Diuum,
  lux autem canae Tethyi restituit,   70
(pace tua fari hic liceat, Ramnusia Virgo,
  namque ego non ullo uera timore tegam,
nec si me infestis discerpent sidera dictis,
  condita quin uere pectoris euoluam)
non his tam laetor rebus quam me afore semper,   75
  afore me a dominae uertice discrucior,
quicum ego, dum uirgo quidem erat muliebribus expers
  unguentis, una uilia multa bibi.
nunc uos optato quas iunxit lumine
    taeda,
  non prius unanimis corpora coniugibus   80

When the Medes produced new sea and when barbarian 45
   Manhood sailed through the middle of Athos.
What hope is there for hair when mountains yield to
    iron?
   Jove, let all the race of Chalybes perish,
And the man who first began to search underground for
    veins
   And to unsheathe case-hardened iron!   50
Disjoined a little before, sister locks were mourning
   My fate, when Ethiopian Memnon's
Sibling beating the air with vibrant pinions appeared,
   Locrian Arsinoë's winged steed,
And lifting me up he flies away through ethereal shade 55
   And lays me down in Venus' chaste lap.
Zephyrion's Lady herself, the Graian settler by
   Canopus' shore, had sent her minion on that errand.
Then, lest alone in the clear heaven's mosaic floor
   The golden crown from Ariadne's brow   60
Should find a place, but that we also might shine forth,
   The votive spoil of a blonde head,
Wet as I was from weeping on the way to the Gods'
    abode,
   The Goddess set me among the old stars as a new.
For between the lights of Virgo and of savage Leo,   65
   Close to Callisto, Lycaon's daughter,
I wheel to my setting, forerunner of the slow Boötes
   Who dives little and late in deep Oceanus.
But though at night the feet of the Gods walk over me
   And daylight returns me to grey Tethys   70
(Here let me speak without offence, Rhamnusian Maid,
   For I shall not hide the truth through any fear,
Not even if the stars tear me apart for slander,
   But truly uncover the secrets of my heart)
I am not so glad of that as tortured because I am parted, 75
   Forever parted, from my Lady's head,
Along with which, while as unwed she forwent all
   Womanly creams, I drank many cheaper ones.
Now you whom wedding-torch's longed-for light has
    joined,
   Yield not your bodies to like-minded mates,   80

tradite nudantes reiecta ueste papillas
    quam iucunda mihi munera libet onyx,
uester onyx casto colitis quae iura cubili.
    sed quae se impuro dedit adulterio,
illius, a, mala dona leuis bibat irrita puluis,   85
    namque ego ab indignis praemia nulla peto.
sed magis, o nuptae, semper concordia uestras,
    semper amor sedes incolat assiduus.
tu uero, regina, tuens cum sidera Diuam
    placabis festis luminibus Venerem,   90
unguinis expertem non siris esse tuam me,
    sed potius largis efficfice muneribus
sidera cur iterent: 'utinam coma regia fiam!
    proximus Hydrochoi fulgeret Oarion!'

LXVII

O dulci iucunda uiro, iucunda parenti,
    salue teque bona Iuppiter auctet ope,
ianua, quam Balbo dicunt seruisse benigne
    olim cum sedes ipse senex tenuit,
quamque ferunt rursus gnato seruisse maligne   5
    postquam es porrecto facta marita sene.
dic agedum nobis quare mutata
      feraris
    in dominum ueterem deseruisse fidem.
'Non (ita Caecilio placeam, cui tradita nunc sum)
    culpa mea est, quamquam dicitur esse mea,   10
nec peccatum a me quisquam pote dicere quicquam
    uere, etsi populi uana loquela facit,
qui, quacumque aliquid reperitur non bene factum,
    ad me omnes clamant: "ianua, culpa tua est".'
Non istuc satis est uno te dicere uerbo,   15
    sed facere ut quiuis sentiat et uideat.
'Qui possum? nemo quaerit nec scire laborat.'
    Nos uolumus. nobis dicere ne dubita.
'Primum igitur, uirgo quod fertur tradita nobis
    falsum est. non illam uir prior attigerat,   20
languidior tenera cui pendens sicula beta
    numquam se mediam sustulit ad tunicam;

Flinging back your robe to show your naked nipples,
  Till onyx pours for me a glad libation,
Onyx of you who honour the rights of a chaste bed.
  But she who gives herself to unclean adultery—
Her evil gifts, ah, null and void let light dust drink,   85
  For I seek no rewards from the unworthy.
But rather, O you brides, may harmony forever,
  Constant love forever dwell in your houses.
And you, Queen, when star-gazing you propitiate
  Divine Venus with festal lights,   90
Suffer me not, your servant, to lack a share of ointment,
  But rather give reason by much largesse
For the stars to repeat 'O were I Berenice's Lock
  Orion could sparkle next Aquarius!'

LXVII

O sweet husband's comfort, parent's comfort, greetings
  And may Jupiter grant you prosperity,
Door, who they say served Balbus loyally in the days
  When that old man was master of the house,
But then, I gather, served his son unkindly, after   5
  The old man was laid out and you got married.
Now come on, tell us why you're rumoured to have
      changed
  And broken faith with your old master.
'So may I please Caecilius, to whom I now belong,
  I'm not to blame, though they say I am.   10
No one can truly say I did anything wrong,
  Though the people's empty gossip does.
For whenever any misdeed comes to light
  They all shout at me "Door, it's your fault".'
It's not enough for you to say that without proof.   15
  Explain to people, make them see it's true.
'How can I? No one asks or takes pains to find out.'
  We want to. Don't hesitate to tell us.
'Well, first, the story that she came to us a virgin
  Is false. Her former husband had not touched her;   20
His bodkin hung more limply than soft beet and never
  Raised itself to his tunic's middle.

sed pater illius gnati uiolasse cubile
    dicitur et miseram conscelerasse domum,
siue quod impia mens caeco flagrabat amore   25
    seu quod iners sterili semine natus erat,
ut quaerendum unde unde foret neruosius illud
    quod posset zonam soluere uirgineam.'
Egregium narras mira pietate parentem,
    qui ipse sui gnati minxerit in gremium.   30
'Atqui non solum hoc dicit se cognitum habere
    Brixia Cycneae supposita speculae,
flauus quam molli praecurrit flumine Mella,
    Brixia Veronae mater amata meae,
sed de Postumio et Corneli narrat
      amore,   35
    cum quibus illa malum fecit adulterium.
dixerit hic aliquis: "qui tu istaec, ianua, nosti,
    cui numquam domini limine abesse licet
nec populum auscultare, sed hic suffixa tigillo
    tantum operire soles aut aperire domum?"   40
saepe illam audiui furtiua uoce loquentem
    solam cum ancillis haec sua flagitia,
nomine dicentem quos diximus, utpote quae mi
    speraret nec linguam esse nec auriculam.
praeterea addebat quendam quem dicere
      nolo   45
    nomine, ne tollat rubra supercilia.
longus homo est, magnas cui lites intulit olim
    falsum mendaci uentre puerperium.'

LXVIII A

Quod mihi fortuna casuque oppressus acerbo
    conscriptum hoc lacrimis mittis epistolium,
naufragum ut eiectum spumantibus aequoris undis
    subleuem et a mortis limine restituam,
quem neque sancta Venus molli requiescere somno   5
    desertum in lecto caelibe perpetitur,
nec ueterum dulci scriptorum carmine Musae
    oblectant, cum mens anxia peruigilat,

But his father violated the son's bed, they say,
  And desecrated the unhappy house,
Either because blind love inflamed his impious mind   25
  Or the son was impotent, his seed barren,
So somehow must be found something more sinewy
  Able to undo a virgin's girdle.'
You're talking of astonishing devotion and the finest
  Of fathers! Peeing in his own son's lap!   30
'And yet this isn't all that's known to her, declares
  Brixia, overlooked by Cycnus' watchtower,
Past whom runs golden Mella with his gentle flow,
  Brixia belovèd mother of my Verona.
She speaks of Postumius and of Cornelius' love, with
    both   35
  Of whom the girl committed wicked adultery.
Here someone may object "Door, how do *you* know this
  When you can never leave your master's threshold
Or listen to the people, but stuck here underneath
  The lintel simply open and close the house?"   40
I often heard her talking in a shifty whisper
  Alone with the maids of these scandals of hers,
Naming the names of those I mentioned, inasmuch
  As she didn't believe I had tongue or ear.
What's more she mentioned someone I don't wish to
    name   45
  In case he raises his red eyebrows.
He's a tall person, ex-defendant in a big lawsuit
  About a false childbirth from a cheating womb.'

LXVIII A

That burdened as you are by Fortune and harsh plight
  You send me this note written in tears—
Will I help a shipwrecked man cast up by foaming waves
  And rescue him from the threshold of death,
One whom holy Venus suffers not to rest   5
  In soft sleep, deserted in a single bed,
Nor can the Muses comfort him with the sweet song
  Of old writers while his troubled mind wakes—

id gratum est mihi, me quoniam tibi dicis amicum,
　muneraque et Musarum hinc petis et Veneris.　　10
sed tibi ne mea sint ignota incommoda, Manli,
　neu me odisse putes hospitis officium,
accipe quis merser fortunae fluctibus ipse,
　ne amplius a misero dona beata petas.
tempore quo primum uestis mihi tradita pura est,　　15
　iucundum cum aetas florida uer ageret,
multa satis lusi. non est Dea nescia nostri
　quae dulcem curis miscet amaritiem.
sed totum hoc studium luctu fraterna mihi mors
　abstulit. o misero frater adempte mihi,　　20
tu mea tu moriens fregisti commoda, frater,
　tecum una tota est nostra sepulta domus,
omnia tecum una perierunt gaudia nostra
　quae tuus in uita dulcis alebat amor.
cuius ego interitu tota de mente fugaui　　25
　haec studia atque omnes delicias animi.
quare, quod scribis Veronae turpe Catullo
　esse quod hic quisquis de meliore nota
frigida deserto tepefactet membra cubili,
　id, Manli, non est turpe, magis miserum est.　　30
ignosces igitur si, quae mihi luctus ademit,
　haec tibi non tribuo munera, cum nequeo.
nam quod scriptorum non magna est copia apud me,
　hoc fit quod Romae uiuimus; illa domus,
illa mihi sedes, illic mea carpitur aetas.　　35
　huc una ex multis capsula me sequitur.
quod cum ita sit, nolim statuas nos mente maligna
　id facere aut animo non satis ingenuo
quod tibi non utriusque petenti copia posta est:
　ultro ego deferrem, copia siqua foret.　　40

LXVIII B

Non possum reticere, Deae, qua me Allius in re
　iuuerit aut quantis iuuerit officiis,
ne fugiens saeclis obliuiscentibus aetas
　illius hoc caeca nocte tegat studium:

This gives me pleasure, as you say I am your friend
   And ask me for gifts both of the Muses and of Venus.   10
But lest you do not know that I have troubles, Manlius,
   And think that I grudge the duty of a guest,
I'll tell you how I too welter in Fortune's waves
   That you may no more ask a wretch for happy gifts.
Since first I was allowed to wear the pure toga,   15
   While flowery prime spent delightful spring,
I played a good deal. Not unaware of us the Goddess
   Who blends sweet bitterness with cares.
But now my brother's death has robbed me of all taste
   For that in grief. O brother, stolen from poor me,   20
You, brother, you in dying have broken my content;
   Our whole house is buried along with you.
All our joys along with you have disappeared,
   Joys which in life your sweet love nourished.
For since his passing I have banished from my mind   25
   Those interests and all frivolity of spirit.
Wherefore, when you write "It is shameful for Catullus
   To be at Verona when this upper-class
Anonymous warms cold limbs in a deserted bed"
   That, Manlius, is more pitiable than shameful.   30
So you will forgive me if I do not grant you gifts
   Which grief has taken away from me—I cannot.
That I have not to hand a great supply of writers
   Is because I live in Rome; my home is there,
There is my base, my life is spent there. Only one   35
   Book-box out of many follows me here.
This being so, I would not wish you to suppose
   Me either mean or disingenuous
For not supplying you with either of your requests:
   I'd grant them unasked, if supply there were.   40

LXVIII B

I cannot be silent, Goddesses, about how Allius
   Helped me and with what kindnesses he helped,
Lest the flight of Time's forgetful generations
   Bury in blind night that concern of his:

sed dicam uobis, uos porro dicite multis   45
  milibus et facite haec charta loquatur anus.
    . . . . .

  notescatque magis mortuus atque magis,
nec tenuem texens sublimis aranea telam
  in deserto Alli nomine opus faciat.   50
nam mihi quam dederit duplex Amathusia curam
  scitis, et in quo me torruerit genere
cum tantum arderem quantum Trinacria rupes
  lymphaque in Oetaeis Malia Thermopylis,
maesta neque assiduo tabescere lumina fletu   55
  cessarent tristique imbre madere genae.
qualis in aerii perlucens uertice montis
  riuus muscoso prosilit e lapide,
qui cum de prona praeceps est ualle uolutus,
  per medium densi transit iter populi,   60
dulce uiatori lasso in sudore leuamen
  cum grauis exustos aestus hiulcat agros,
ac uelut in nigro iactatis turbine nautis
  lenius aspirans aura secunda uenit
iam prece Pollucis, iam Castoris implorata,   65
  tale fuit nobis Allius auxilium.
is clausum lato patefecit limite campum,
  isque domum nobis isque dedit dominae,
ad quam communes exerceremus amores,
  quo mea se molli candida diua pede   70
intulit et trito fulgentem in limine plantam
  innixa arguta constituit solea,
coniugis ut quondam flagrans aduenit amore
  Protesilaëam Laodamia domum
inceptam frustra, nondum cum sanguine sacro   75
  hostia Caelestis pacificasset Eros.
(nil mihi tam ualde placeat, Ramnusia Virgo,
  quod temere inuitis suscipiatur Eris!)
quam ieiuna pium desideret ara cruorem
  docta est amisso Laodamia uiro,   80
coniugis ante coacta noui dimittere collum
  quam ueniens una atque altera rursus hiems
noctibus in longis auidum saturasset amorem,
  posset ut abrupto uiuere coniugio,

But I shall tell you; you in turn tell many thousands   45
    And make this paper speak in its old age.
      . . . . .

    And he be more and more famous in death,
Nor spider weaving high in air her slender web
    Work upon Allius' forsaken name.   50
For you know what trouble the two-faced Amathusian
    Brought me and in what manner scorched me
When I was burning hot as the Trinacrian rock
    And Malis' spring in Oetéan Thermopylae,
And my sad eyes were wasted with continual weeping   55
    And my cheeks drenched in bitter showers.
As on the top of an airy mountain glinting
    A stream leaps down from mossy stone
And tumbling headlong down a steep ravine
    Crosses a highway crowded with people,   60
A sweet relief for weary sweating wayfarers
    When burnt fields gape in heavy heat;
And as, for sailors buffeted by a black storm,
    A following wind comes, blowing gently,
Answering their prayers to Pollux and to Castor,   65
    Such help was Allius to us.
He opened a fenced field with a broad bridle-path,
    He gave me and my mistress a house,
Under whose roof we could engage in shared love,
    Where my radiant goddess with soft step   70
Drew near and rested a dazzling foot on the worn sill,
    Pressing it with creaking sandal,
As in the past ablaze with love for a husband came
    Laodamia to the house Protesilaus
Began in vain because no victim's sacred blood   75
    Had yet appeased the Lords of Heaven.
(May nothing please me so strongly, Rhamnusian Maid,
    That is rashly started without those Lords' consent!)
How the famished altar craves blood-sacrifice
    Laodamia learnt from her man's loss,   80
Forced to let go of her new husband's neck before
    The coming of one and another winter
Had satisfied in the long nights love's hunger so
    That she could live with a broken marriage,

quod scibant Parcae non longo tempore abesse   85
   si miles muros isset ad Iliacos.
nam tum Helenae raptu primores Argiuorum
   coeperat ad sese Troia ciere uiros,
Troia (nefas!) commune sepulcrum Asiae Europaeque,
   Troia uirum et uirtutum omnium acerba cinis,   90
quaene etiam nostro letum miserabile fratri
   attulit. ei misero frater adempte mihi,
ei misero fratri iucundum lumen ademptum,
   tccum una tota cst nostra scpulta domus,
omnia tecum una perierunt gaudia nostra   95
   quae tuus in uita dulcis alebat amor.
quem nunc tam longe non inter nota sepulcra
   nec prope cognatos compositum cineres,
sed Troia obscena, Troia infelice sepultum
   detinet extremo terra aliena solo.   100
ad quam tum properans fertur lecta undique pubes
   Graeca penetralis deseruisse focos,
ne Paris abducta gauisus libera moecha
   otia pacato degeret in thalamo.
quo tibi tum casu, pulcerrima Laodamia,   105
   ereptum est uita dulcius atque anima
coniugium: tanto te absorbens uertice
     amoris
   aestus in abruptum detulerat barathrum,
quale ferunt Grai Pheneum prope Cyllenaeum
   siccare emulsa pingue palude solum,   110
quod quondam caesis montis fodisse medullis
   audit falsiparens Amphitryoniades,
tempore quo certa Stymphalia monstra
     sagitta
   perculit imperio deterioris eri,
pluribus ut caeli tereretur ianua Diuis,   115
   Hebe nec longa uirginitate foret.
sed tuus altus amor barathro fuit altior illo,
   qui tamen indomitam ferre iugum docuit.
nam nec tam carum confecto aetate parenti
   una caput seri nata nepotis alit,   120
qui, cum diuitiis uix tandem inuentus auitis
   nomen testatas intulit in tabulas,

Which the Parcae knew was not a long time off   85
   If he went soldiering to Ilium's walls.
For it was then, on Helen's rape, that Troy began
   To rouse against herself the chief men of the Argives,
Troy (horror!), common grave of Europe and of Asia,
   Troy, bitter ash of men and every manly virtue!   90
Did she not bring our brother also pitiable
   Doom? Alas, brother, stolen from poor me,
Alas, poor brother, robbed of the cheerful light!
   Our whole house is buried along with you.
All our joys along with you have disappeared,   95
   Joys which in life your sweet love nourished,
Who now so far away and not among familiar
   Graves nor laid to rest near kindred ashes,
But buried at Troy the obscene, at disastrous Troy,
   Are held by an alien land in distant soil.   100
Thither then hurrying, picked warriors from all Greece
   Are said to have forsaken hearth and home
Lest Paris freely enjoying the adulteress he stole
   Should spend his leisure in her bower at peace.
Thus it befell, most beautiful Laodamia,   105
   That you were robbed then of a husband sweeter
Than life and breath: with such a current sucking you
     down,
   Love's tide had plunged you in a sheer abyss,
Like that the Greeks report near Cyllenéan Pheneus
   As draining dry the fat soil of a swamp,   110
Which once false-fathered Amphitryóniades is fabled
   To have dug while cutting into a mountain's marrow
What time he shot with sure-aimed arrow those
     Stymphalian
   Monsters at his inferior lord's command,
That Heaven's gateway might be trodden by more Gods   115
   Nor Hebe have a long virginity.
But your deep love was deeper than that famed abyss
   And taught you, though untamed, to bear the yoke.
For not so dear to parent spent with age the head
   Of late-born grandson nursed by an only daughter,   120
Who, lighted on at long last for grandfather's fortune,
   His name inserted in the witnessed will,

impia derisi gentilis gaudia tollens
    suscitat a cano uolturium capiti;
nec tantum niueo gauisa est ulla columbo   125
    compar, quae multo dicitur improbius
oscula mordenti semper decerpere rostro
    quam quae praecipue multiuola est mulier.
sed tu horum magnos uicisti sola furores
    ut semel es flauo conciliata uiro.   130
aut nihil aut paulo cui tum concedere digna
    lux mea se nostrum contulit in grcmium,
quam circumcursans hinc illinc saepe Cupido
    fulgebat crocina candidus in tunica.
quae tamen etsi uno non est contenta Catullo,   135
    rara uerecundae furta feremus erae,
ne nimium simus stultorum more molesti.
    saepe etiam Iuno, maxima Caelicolum,
coniugis in culpa flagrantem contudit iram,
    noscens Omniuoli plurima furta Iouis.   140
atqui nec Diuis homines componier aequum est
    (ingratum tremuli tolle parentis onus!)
nec tamen illa mihi dextra deducta paterna
    fragrantem Assyrio uenit odore domum,
sed furtiua dedit mira munuscula nocte   145
    ipsius ex ipso dempta uiri gremio.
quare illud satis est si nobis is datur unis
    quem lapide illa diem candidiore notat.

Hoc tibi, quod potui, confectum carmine munus
    pro multis, Alli, redditur officiis,   150
ne uestrum scabra tangat rubigine nomen
    haec atque illa dies atque alia atque alia.
huc addent Diui quam plurima quae Themis olim
    antiquis solita est munera ferre piis.
sitis felices et tu simul et tua uita,   155
    et domus in qua nos lusimus et domina,
et qui principio nobis te tradidit, Afer
    a quo sunt primo mi omnia nata bona,
et longe ante omnes mihi quae me carior ipso est,
    lux mea, qua uiua uiuere dulce mihi est.   160

Ends the ungodly joy of a fooled distant kinsman
   And shoos the vulture from the white-haired head.
Neither has any dove so much enjoyed her snowy   125
   Consort, though she is said more shamelessly by far
To gather kisses with an ever nipping beak
   Than even the willingest of women.
But you alone exceeded the mad passion of these
   When once united with your fair-haired man.   130
Deserving to yield nothing or but little to her,
   My light on that day gave herself to our lap
And often Cupid running here and there about her
   Gleamed dazzling in a saffron tunic.
Yet though she is not satisfied with one Catullus   135
   We shall bear the rare thefts of a discreet lady,
Lest like the stupid we are too much of a nuisance.
   Even Juno, greatest of Heaven's Dwellers, has often
Fought down blazing anger at her husband's fault,
   Learning of the many thefts of All-Willing Jove.   140
But neither is it right to liken men to Gods
   (Take up the ungrateful burden of an anxious parent!)
Nor yet did she come to me upon her father's arm
   To a house fragrant with Assyrian perfume,
But on a wondrous night gave stolen little gifts   145
   Taken from the very lap of her very husband.
Wherefore it is enough if I alone am given
   The day she marks with a whiter stone.

This gift achieved in song (all I could manage), Allius,
   Is sent you in return for many kindnesses,   150
Lest this and the next day and another and another
   Should touch your name with rust's corrosion.
The Gods will add to it those many gifts that Themis
   In old days used to bring the faithful.
May you be happy both, you and your life, together,   155
   And the house I and my mistress played in,
And Afer, the one who introduced you to us first,
   With whom all my good things originate,
And she beyond all, far dearer to me than my own self,
   My light, whose life makes living sweet for me.   160

LXIX

Noli admirari quare tibi femina nulla,
  Rufe, uelit tenerum supposuisse femur,
non si illam rarae labefactes munere uestis
  aut perluciduli deliciis lapidis.
laedit te quaedam mala fabula, qua tibi fertur   5
  ualle sub alarum trux habitare caper.
hunc metuunt omnes. neque mirum: nam mala ualde est
  bestia nec quicum bella puella cubet.
quare aut crudelem nasorum interfice pestem
  aut admirari desine cur fugiunt.   10

LXX

Nulli se dicit mulier mea nubere malle
  quam mihi, non si se Iuppiter ipse petat.
dicit—sed mulier cupido quod dicit amanti
  in uento et rapida scribere oportet aqua.

LXXI

Sicui iure bono sacer alarum obstitit hircus
  aut siquem merito tarda podagra secat,
aemulus iste tuus qui uestrum exercet amorem
  mirifice est apte nactus utrumque malum.
nam quotiens futuit, totiens ulciscitur ambos: 5
  illam affligit odore; ipse perit podagra.

LXXII

Dicebas quondam solum te nosse Catullum,
  Lesbia, nec prae me uelle tenere Iouem.
dilexi tum te non tantum ut uulgus
     amicam
  sed pater ut gnatos diligit et generos.
nunc te cognoui. quare etsi impensius uror,   5
  multo mi tamen es uilior et leuior.
'qui potis est?' inquis? quod amantem iniuria
     talis
  cogit amare magis sed bene uelle minus.

LXIX

You should not wonder, Rufus, why no woman
   Wants to lay her soft thigh under you,
Even though you tempt her with a gift of rare fabric
   Or the treat of a translucent stone.
Your trouble is a nasty rumour, which reports   5
   You feed a fierce goat down in Arm-Pit Valley.
He scares them all. No wonder. It's a very nasty
   Brute no pretty girl would go to bed with.
So either kill this cruel scourge of noses
   Or cease to wonder why they run away.   10

LXX

My woman says there's no one she would rather wed
   Than me, not even if asked by Jove himself.
Says—but what a woman says to an eager lover
   One should write on the wind and the running water.

LXXI

If the curst arm-pit goat rightly harmed anyone
   Or hobbling gout deservedly torments,
That rival of yours who works away at your shared love
   Has caught both troubles wonderfully aptly.
Each time he fucks he punishes the pair of them—   5
   Sickens her with stench and kills himself with gout.

LXXII

You said one day you only knew Catullus, Lesbia,
   And you'd refuse to embrace even Jove instead of me.
I loved you then, not only as common men their girl-
     friend
   But as a father loves his sons and sons-in-law.
I know you now. So though my passion's more intense,   5
   Yet for me you're much cheaper and lighter-weight.
'How can that be?' you ask. It's because such hurt
     compels
   A lover to love more but to like less.

LXXIII

Desine de quoquam quicquam bene uelle mereri
  aut aliquem fieri posse putare pium.
omnia sunt ingrata. nihil fecisse benigne
  prodest. immo etiam taedet obestque magis,
ut mihi, quem nemo grauius nec acerbius
    urget   5
    quam modo qui me unum atque unicum amicum
    habuit.

LXXIV

Gellius audicrat patruum obiurgare solere
  siquis delicias diceret aut faceret.
hoc ne ipsi accideret patrui perdepsuit ipsam
  uxorem et patruum reddidit Harpocratem.
quod uoluit fecit: nam quamuis irrumet ipsum   5
  nunc patruum, uerbum non faciet patruus.

LXXV

Huc est mens deducta tua mea, Lesbia, culpa
  atque ita se officio perdidit ipsa suo,
ut iam nec bene uelle queat tibi, si optima fias,
  nec desistere amare, omnia si facias.

LXXVI

Siqua recordanti benefacta priora uoluptas
  est homini cum se cogitat esse pium
ncc sanctam uiolassc fidcm ncc foedere in ullo
  Diuum ad fallendos numine abusum homines,
multa parata manent in longa aetate, Catulle,   5
  ex hoc ingrato gaudia amore tibi.
nam quaecumque homines bene cuiquam aut dicere
    possunt
    aut facere, haec a te dictaque factaque sunt.
omnia quae ingratae perierunt credita menti.
    quare iam te cur amplius excrucies?   10

LXXIII

Stop wanting to earn any thanks from anyone
   Or thinking someone can prove true.
Ingratitude is all. Kindness counts for nothing.
   No, it's even tiresome and does harm,
As I have found, whom no one pushes harder or more
    harshly   5
   Than he who lately called me 'one and only
    friend'.

LXXIV

Gellius had heard that uncle liked to reprimand
   Any who spoke or acted naughtily.
To avoid this for himself he massaged uncle's wife,
   Turned uncle into an Harpocrates
And thus achieved his aim. For were he now to stuff   5
   Uncle himself, uncle won't say a word.

LXXV

Lesbia, my will has sunk to this through your frailty
   And so destroyed itself by its own kindness
That it could neither like you, even were you perfect,
   Nor cease to love you though you stopped at nothing.

LXXVI

If in recalling former kindnesses there's pleasure
   When a man reflects that he has been true
Nor broken solemn promise nor in any pact
   Abused the Gods' goodwill to fool his fellow men,
Then many joys remain in store for you, Catullus,   5
   Through a long lifetime from this ungrateful love.
For whatever kind things men can say or
    do
   To anyone, these you have said and done,
But credited to ingratitude they have all been wasted.
   So now why torture yourself any more?   10

quin tu animum offirmas atque istinc teque reducis
   et Dis inuitis desinis esse miser?
difficile est longum subito deponere amorem.
   difficile est, uerum hoc qualubet efficias.
una salus haec est. hoc est tibi peruincendum.   15
   hoc facias, siue id non pote siue pote.
o Di, si uestrum est misereri aut si quibus umquam
   extremam iam ipsa in morte tulistis opem,
me miserum aspicite et, si uitam puriter egi,
   eripite hanc pestem perniciemque mihi,   20
quae mihi subrepens imos ut torpor in artus
   expulit ex omni pectore laetitias.
non iam illud quaero, contra me ut diligat illa,
   aut, quod non potis est, esse pudica uelit.
ipse ualere opto et taetrum hunc deponere morbum.   25
   o Di, reddite mi hoc pro pietate mea.

LXXVII

Rufe, mihi frustra ac nequiquam credite amice,
   (frustra? immo magno cum pretio atque malo)
sicine subrepsti mi atque intestina perurens
   ei misero eripuisti omnia nostra bona?
eripuisti, eheu nostrae crudele uenenum   5
   uitae, eheu nostrae pestis amicitiae.

LXXVIII

Gallus habet fratres, quorum est lepidissima coniunx
   alterius, lepidus filius alterius.
Gallus homo est bellus: nam dulces iungit amores,
   cum puero ut bello bella puella cubet.
Gallus homo est stultus, nec se uidet esse maritum   5
   qui patruus patrui monstret adulterium.

LXXVIII B

. . . . .

sed nunc id doleo, quod purae pura puellae
   suauia comminxit spurca saliua tua.

Why not harden your heart and tear yourself away
   And stop being wretched against the Gods' will?
It's difficult to break with long love suddenly.
   It's difficult, but this you must somehow do.
This is your only chance. You must win through to this.   15
   Possible or not, this you must achieve.
O Gods, if you can pity or have ever brought
   Help at last to any on the point of death,
Look on my wretchedness and if I have led a decent life
   Take away from me this deadly disease,   20
Which like a paralysis creeping into my inmost being
   Has driven from my heart every happiness.
I do not ask now that she love me in return
   Or, what's impossible, that she be chaste.
I pray for my own health, to be rid of this foul sickness.   25
   O Gods, grant me this for my true dealing.

LXXVII

Rufus, believed my friend in vain and all for nothing,
   (For nothing? No, to my great cost and sorrow)
Is this how you've crept up on me, burnt through my guts
   And robbed poor me of all I value?
Yes, you've robbed me, alas, cruel poison of our life,   5
   Alas, the canker on our friendship.

LXXVIII

Gallus has brothers, one with an attractive son,
   The other with a most attractive wife.
Gallus is nice. He brings sweet loves together
   So that nice girl can bed down with nice boy.
Gallus is stupid—can't see he's a married   5
   Uncle teaching cuckoldry of uncle.

LXXVIII B

. . . . .

But now what riles me is that your disgusting spittle
   Has piddled on a pure girl's pure kisses.

uerum id non impune feres, nam te omnia saecla
   noscent et qui sis fama loquetur anus.

LXXIX

Lesbius est pulcer. quid ni? quem Lesbia malit
   quam te cum tota gente, Catulle, tua.
sed tamen hic pulcer uendat cum gente
      Catullum
   si tria notorum suauia reppererit.

LXXX

Quid dicam, Gelli, quare rosea ista labella
   hiberna fiant candidiora niue
mane domo cum exis et cum te octaua
      quiete
   e molli longo suscitat hora die?
nescioquid certe est. an uere fama
      susurrat
   grandia te medii tenta uorare uiri?
sic certe est. clamant Victoris rupta miselli
   ilia et emulso labra notata sero.

5

LXXXI

Nemone in tanto potuit populo esse, Iuuenti,
   bellus homo quem tu diligere inciperes
praeterquam iste tuus moribunda ab sede Pisauri
   hospes inaurata pallidior statua
qui tibi nunc cordi est, quem tu praeponere
      nobis
   audes et nescis quod facinus facias?

5

LXXXII

Quinti, si tibi uis oculos debere Catullum
   aut aliud siquid carius est oculis,
eripere ei noli multo quod carius illi
   est oculis seu quid carius est oculis.

You'll pay for that, though. Every century shall know you
   And Fame in old age tell what sort you are.

LXXIX

Lesbius is handsome. Of course, for Lesbia prefers him
   To you and all your clan, Catullus. But
Handsome is welcome to sell Catullus and his clan as
     slaves
   If he can get three kisses from those who know him.

LXXX

Gellius, how explain why those red lips of yours
   Show whiter than the winter snow
Both when you leave home early and when the long day's
    eighth
   Hour rouses you from gentle rest?
Surely there's something wrong? Is Rumour's whisper
   true?   5
   You mouth big stretchings of mid-male?
It must be so. Poor Victor's ruptured groin shouts it
   And those lips marked with milked-out whey.

LXXXI

Among so many people was there really no 'nice man',
   Juventius, for you to fall in love with
Except that guest of yours from moribund Pisaurum
   More jaundiced than a gilded statue,
Who tickles your present fancy, whom you dare prefer to
   us   5
   Not knowing what a shocker you are making?

LXXXII

Quintius, if you wish Catullus to owe you his eyes
   Or anything more precious than eyes,
Don't rob him of what's far more precious than his eyes
   Or than anything more precious than eyes.

LXXXIII

Lesbia mi praesente uiro mala plurima dicit:
   haec illi fatuo maxima laetitia est.
mule, nihil sentis. si nostri oblita taceret,
   sana esset: nunc quod gannit et obloquitur,
non solum meminit sed, quae multo acrior est
     res,   5
   irata est. hoc est, uritur et loquitur.

LXXXIV

Chommoda dicebat siquando commoda uellet
   dicere, et insidias Arrius hinsidias,
et tum mirifice sperabat se esse locutum
   cum quantum poterat dixerat hinsidias.
credo sic matcr, sic liber auunculus eius,   5
   sic maternus auus dixerat atque auia.
hoc misso in Syriam requierant omnibus aures;
   audibant eadem haec leniter et
      leuiter,
nec sibi postilla metuebant talia uerba,
   cum subito affertur nuntius horribilis: 10
Ionios fluctus, postquam illuc Arrius isset,
   iam non Ionios esse sed Hionios.

LXXXV

Odi et amo. quare id faciam fortasse requiris?
   nescio sed fieri sentio et excrucior.

LXXXVI

Quintia formosa est multis; mihi candida, longa,
   recta est. haec ego sic singula confiteor.
totum illud 'formosa' nego. nam nulla uenustas,
   nulla in tam magno est corpore mica salis.
Lesbia formosa est, quae cum pulcerrima tota est, 5
   tum omnibus una omnis surripuit ueneres.

LXXXIII

In husband's presence Lesbia keeps abusing me,
  Which makes that silly man extremely happy.
Mule, you've no sense. If she forgot me and kept quiet,
  She'd be heart-whole, but nagging talk against me
Means she remembers and, what's much more to the
    point,   5
  Is riled. In other words, she burns and talks.

LXXXIV

'Hemoluments' said Arrius, meaning to say
  'Emoluments' and 'hambush' meaning 'ambush',
Hoping that he had spoken most impressively
  When he said 'hambush' with great emphasis.
His mother, her free-born brother and his maternal   5
  Grandparents, I believe, all spoke like that.
Posted to Syria he gave the ears of all a rest.
  They heard the same words smoothly and gently
    spoken
And had no fear thenceforward of such aspirates,
  When suddenly there came the frightful news   10
That after Arrius arrived the Ionian waves,
  Ionian no more, became 'Hionian'.

LXXXV

I hate and love. Perhaps you're asking why I do that?
  I don't know, but I feel it happening, and am racked.

LXXXVI

For many Quintia's beautiful; for me she's fair,
  Tall, straight. I grant these separate points,
But not that wholeness 'beauty'. For she has no charm,
  No grain of salt in that great body.
Now Lesbia's beautiful, wholly most lovely, and alone 5
  She has robbed them all of all their charms.

LXXXVII

Nulla potest mulier tantum se dicere amatam
   uere quantum a me Lesbia amata mea est.
nulla fides ullo fuit umquam in foedere tanta
   quanta in amore tuo ex parte reperta mea est.

LXXXVIII

Quid facit is, Gelli, qui cum matre atque
    sorore
   prurit et abiectis peruigilat tunicis?
quid facit is patruum qui non sinit esse maritum?
   ecquid scis quantum suscipiat sceleris?
suscipit, o Gelli, quantum non ultima
    Tethys   5
   nec genitor Nympharum abluit Oceanus.
nam nihil est quicquam sceleris quo prodeat ultra,
   non si demisso se ipse uoret capite.

LXXXIX

Gellius est tenuis. quid ni? cui tam bona
    mater
   tamque ualens uiuat tamque uenusta soror
tamque bonus patruus tamque omnia plena
    puellis
   cognatis, quare is desinat esse macer?
qui ut nihil attingat nisi quod fas tangere non
    est,   5
   quantumuis quare sit macer inuenies.

XC

Nascatur magus ex Gelli matrisque
    nefando
   coniugio et discat Persicum haruspicium.
nam magus ex matre et gnato gignatur oportet,
   si uera est Persarum impia religio,

LXXXVII

No woman can say truly she has been loved as much
  As Lesbia mine has been loved by me.
No faith so great was ever found in any contract
  As on my part in love of you.

LXXXVIII

Gellius, what does he do who lusts with mother and
    sister
  And flinging off tunic stays awake all night?
What does he do who won't let uncle be a husband?
  Do you know how great a crime he commits?
He commits, O Gellius, one which neither furthest
    Tethys   5
  Nor Ocean, Sire of Nymphs, can wash away.
Beyond that there's no worse crime he could perpetrate,
  Not if head down he were to mouth himself.

LXXXIX

Gellius is slender. Of course. His mother's so kind and so
    fit
  And his sister so attractive
And his uncle so kind and the whole place so full of
    female cousins,
  Why should he stop being thin?
Even if he touches nothing but what it's forbidden to
    touch,   5
  You'll find there's plenty cause to keep him thin.

XC

Let a Mage be born of Gellius and his mother's impious
    mating
  And let him learn Persian haruspicy.
For the future Mage must be offspring of mother and son,
  If the Persians' unholy religion is true,

gratus ut accepto ueneretur carmine
   Diuos   5
omentum in flamma pingue liquefaciens.

XCI

Non ideo, Gelli, sperabam te mihi fidum
   in misero hoc nostro, hoc perdito amore fore
quod te cognossem bene constantemue putarem
   aut posse a turpi mentem inhibere probro,
sed neque quod matrem nec germanam esse uidebam 5
   hanc tibi cuius me magnus edebat amor.
et quamuis tecum multo coniungerer usu,
   non satis id causae credideram esse tibi.
tu satis id duxti. tantum tibi gaudium in omni
   culpa est, in quacumque est aliquid sceleris.   10

XCII

Lesbia mi dicit semper male nec tacet umquam
   de me. Lesbia me dispeream nisi amat.
quo signo? quia sunt totidem mea. deprecor illam
   assidue, uerum dispeream nisi amo.

XCIII

Nil nimium studeo, Caesar, tibi uelle placere
   nec scire utrum sis albus an ater homo.

XCIV

Mentula moechatur. 'moechatur mentula?' certe.
   hoc est quod dicunt: 'ipsa olera olla legit.'

XCV

Zmyrna mei Cinnae nonam post denique messem
   quam coepta est nonamque edita post hiemem,
milia cum interea quingenta Hortensius uno
      . . . . .

So he can gratefully worship the Gods with acceptable
   chant   5
  As he melts the fat caul in the flames.

XCI

I hoped you would be loyal to me, Gellius,
  In this wretched, this desperate love of ours,
Not as I knew you well or thought you trustworthy
  Or able to keep your thoughts from lewdness,
But as I saw that she for whom great love was eating me   5
  Was neither your mother nor your sister.
And though I had for long been intimate with you,
  I doubted you'd find that sufficient motive.
And yet you did. So great is your delight in any
  Offence with something criminal about it.   10

XCII

Lesbia's always abusing me and can't keep quiet
  About me. I'm damned if Lesbia doesn't love me.
The proof? Because I'm just the same—forever praying
  To be rid of her, but I'm damned if I don't love her.

XCIII

I am none too keen to wish to please you, Caesar,
  Nor to know if you're a white man or a black.

XCIV

TOOL is adulterous. 'Adulterous, Tool?' Of course.
  It's like they say: *The pot picks its own parsnips*.

XCV

Zmyrna, my Cinna's, brought forth at last, nine harvests
  And nine winters after her inception!
Meanwhile Hortensius five hundred thousand in one
     . . . . .

Zmyrna cauas Satrachi penitus mittetur ad undas;   5
    Zmyrnam cana diu saecula peruoluent.
at Volusi Annales Paduam morientur ad ipsam
    et laxas scombris saepe dabunt tunicas.
parua mei mihi sunt cordi monumenta sodalis;
    at populus tumido gaudeat Antimacho.   10

XCVI

Si quicquam mutis gratum acceptumue sepulcris
    accidere a nostro, Calue, dolore potest,
quo desiderio ueteres renouamus amores
    atque olim missas flemus amicitias,
certe non tanto mors immatura dolori est   5
    Quintiliae quantum gaudet amore tuo.

XCVII

Non (ita me Di ament) quicquam referre putaui
    utrumne os an culum olfacerem Aemilio,
nilo mundius hoc nihiloque immundius illud.
    uerum etiam culus mundior et melior,
nam sine dentibus est. os dentis sesquipedalis,   5
    gingiuas uero ploxeni habet ueteris,
praeterea rictum qualem diffissus in aestu
    meientis mulae cunnus habere solet.
hic futuit multas et se facit esse uenustum,
    et non pistrino traditur atque asino?   10
quem siqua attingit, non illam posse putemus
    aegroti culum lingere carnificis?

XCVIII

In te, si in quemquam, dici pote, putide Victi,
    id quod uerbosis dicitur et fatuis.
ista cum lingua, si usus ueniat tibi,
        possis
    culos et crepidas lingere carpatinas.
si nos omnino uis omnes perdere, Victi,   5
    hiscas; omnino quod cupis efficies.

Zmyrna will travel far—to Satrachus' sunken waves; 5
   Long will the white-haired centuries read *Zmyrna*.
Volusius' *Annals*, though, will die beside the Padua
   And often make loose jackets for mackerel.
Dear to my heart is my comrade's small-scale monument;
   The crowd can admire long-winded Antimachus. 10

XCVI

If anything grateful or welcome, Calvus, can befall
   The silent tomb from grief of ours,
From the longing with which we relive old loves
   And weep for past friendships thrown away,
Quintilia surely feels less grief at untimely death 5
   Than gladness for your love.

XCVII

I thought (so help me Gods!) it made no difference
   Whether I smelt Aemilius' mouth or arsehole,
One being no cleaner, the other no filthier.
   But in fact the arsehole's cleaner and kinder:
It has no teeth. The mouth has teeth half-a-yard long 5
   And gums like an ancient wagon-chassis.
Moreover when it opens up it's like the cunt
   Of a pissing mule dehiscent in a heat-wave.
And he fucks many girls and fancies himself a charmer
   And isn't sent down to the mill and its moke? 10
Wouldn't one think that any woman who touched *him*
   Could lick the arsehole of a sick hangman?

XCVIII

Of you, if of anyone, stinking Victius, can be said
   What's said to windbags and the absurd.
With a tongue like that you could, if you should have
    occasion,
   Lick arseholes and farm-labourers' boots.
If you wish to lose us all altogether, Victius, 5
   Just open your mouth; you'll be altogether successful.

XCIX

Surripui tibi dum ludis, mellite
    Iuuenti,
  suauiolum dulci dulcius ambrosia.
uerum id non impune tuli, namque amplius horam
  suffixum in summa me memini esse cruce
dum tibi me purgo nec possum fletibus ullis   5
  tantillum uestrae demere saeuitiae.
nam simul id factum est, multis diluta labella
  guttis abstersti mollibus articulis
ne quicquam nostro contractum ex ore manerct,
  tamquam commictae spurca saliua lupae.   10
praeterea infesto miserum me tradere amori
  non cessasti omnique excruciare modo,
ut mi ex ambrosia mutatum iam foret illud
  suauiolum tristi tristius helleboro.
quam quoniam poenam misero proponis amanti,   15
  numquam iam posthac basia surripiam.

C

Caelius Aufillenum et Quintius Aufillenam
  flos Veronensum depereunt iuuenum,
hic fratrem, ille sororem. hoc est, quod dicitur, illud
  fraternum uere dulce sodalicium.
cui faueam potius? Caeli, tibi, nam tua nobis   5
  perspecta est igni tum unica amicitia
cum uesana meas torreret flamma medullas.
  sis felix, Caeli; sis in amore potens.

CI

Multas per gentes et multa per aequora uectus
  aduenio has miseras, frater, ad inferias,
ut te postremo donarem munere mortis
  ct mutam nequiquam alloquerer cinerem,
quandoquidem fortuna mihi tete abstulit ipsum,   5
  heu miser indigne frater adempte mihi.

XCIX

Honeyed Juventius, while you were playing I stole from
    you
    A sweeter kiss than sweet ambrosia.
Yes, but I didn't get it scot-free, for I remember
    Being stuck for more than an hour on a cross
While I made my excuses to you but could not move   5
    Your cruelty one bit with all my tears.
For hardly was it done before you drenched your lips
    With water-drops and wiped them with soft knuckles,
Lest anything infectious from my mouth remain,
    As though it were some pissed-on whore's foul spittle.   10
Besides you were not slow to hand wretched me over
    To angry Love and crucify me every way,
So that for me that kiss was now turned from ambrosia
    To something sourer than sour hellebore.
Since you propose this penalty for a wretched lover,   15
    Henceforth I'll never steal a kiss again.

C

Caelius and Quintius, flower of Verona's youth,
    Have fallen for Aufillenus and Aufillena,
One for the brother, the other for the sister. Truly this
    Is the 'sweet sibling bond' they talk of.
Which shall I favour? Caelius, you, because your special   5
    Friendship for me was proved by fire in the days
When the demented flame was shrivelling my marrow.
    Caelius, good luck! May you be capable of love.

CI

Travelling through many nations and through many seas
    I have come, brother, for these poor funeral rites,
That I might render you the last dues of the dead
    And vainly comfort your dumb ashes,
Because Fortune has robbed me of your self, alas,   5
    Poor brother, unfairly taken from me.

nunc tamen interea haec prisco quae more
    parentum
  tradita sunt tristi munere ad inferias
accipe fraterno multum manantia fletu,
    atquc in perpetuum, frater, aue atque uale.   10

CII

Si quoiquam tacitum commissum est fido ab amico,
    cuius sit penitus nota fides animi,
meque esse inucnics illorum iure sacratum,
    Corneli, et factum me esse, puta, Harpocratem.

CIII

Aut sodes mihi redde decem sestertia, Silo,
    deinde esto quamuis saeuus et indomitus,
aut, si te nummi delectant, desine quaeso
    leno esse atque idem saeuus et indomitus.

CIV

Credis me potuisse meae maledicere uitae,
    ambobus mihi quae carior est oculis?
non potui, nec si possem tam perdite amarem.
    sed tu cum Tappone omnia monstra facis.

CV

Mentula conatur Pipleium scandere montem:
    Musae furcillis praecipitem eiciunt.

CVI

Cum puero bello praeconem qui uidet esse,
    quid credat nisi se uendere discupere?

But now, meanwhile, accept these gifts which by old
    custom
Of the ancestors are offered in sad duty
At funeral rites, gifts drenched in a brother's tears,
    And forever, brother, greetings and farewell.   10

CII

If faithful friend entrusted secret to anyone
    Whose own good faith was fully known,
You'll find me too, Cornelius, devoted to their rule
    And turned into, let's say, Harpocrates.

CIII

Either please pay me back the ten *sestertia*, Silo,
    Then be as savage and high-handed as you like,
Or, if the money takes your fancy, kindly stop
    Being a pimp who's savage and high-handed.

CIV

Do you believe I could have cursed my life
    Who's dearer to me than both eyes?
I could not. If I could I wouldn't love so desperately.
    But you and Tappo are up to every enormity.

CV

TOOL tries to scale the Mount of Pipla:
    Muses with pitchforks throw him down.

CVI

Seeing an auctioneer with a pretty boy
    One can't but think he wants to sell himself.

CVII

Si quicquam cupido optantique optigit umquam
    insperanti, hoc est gratum animo proprie.
quare hoc est gratum nobis quoque—carius auro
    quod te restituis, Lesbia, mi cupido.
restituis cupido atque insperanti, ipsa refers
      te   5
    nobis. o lucem candidiore nota!
quis me uno uiuit felicior, aut magis hac re
    optandum in uita dicere quis poterit?

CVIII

Si, Comini, populi arbitrio tua cana senectus
    spurcata impuris moribus intereat,
non equidem dubito quin primum inimica bonorum
    lingua exsecta auido sit data uulturio,
effossos oculos uoret atro gutture coruus,   5
    intestina canes, cetera membra lupi.

CIX

Iucundum, mea uita, mihi proponis amorem
    hunc nostrum inter nos perpetuumque fore.
Di magni, facite ut uere promittere possit
    atque id sincere dicat et ex animo,
ut liceat nobis tota perducere uita   5
    aeternum hoc sanctae foedus amicitiae.

CX

Aufillena, bonae semper laudantur amicae:
    accipiunt pretium quae facere instituunt.
tu, quod promisti mihi quod mentita, inimica es,
    quod nec das et fers saepe, facis facinus.
aut facere ingenuae est aut non promisse pudicae,   5
    Aufillena, fuit; sed data corripere
fraudando est furis—plus quam meretricis auarae
    quae sese toto corpore prostituit.

CVII

If anything wished or prayed for ever happened to anyone
　Unexpectedly, that can truly be thought welcome.
And so for us too it is welcome, more precious than gold,
　That you give yourself back to me, Lesbia, as I wished.
Give yourself back as I wished, unexpectedly, bring
　　yourself back　　　　　　　　　　　　　　　　　5
　To us willingly. O daylight of luckier mark!
Who in the world lives happier than I? Or who can say
　What's more to be prayed for in life than this?

CVIII

Cominius, if the people's will were to put an end to
　Your old age, grey and foul with filthy morals,
I have no doubt that first your tongue, all good men's foe,
　Would be cut out and given to a greedy vulture;
A black-throat crow would dig out and devour your eyes,　5
　Dogs your intestines, wolves your other parts.

CIX

You give me hope this mutual love of ours, my life,
　Will be delightful and for ever.
Great Gods, enable her to promise truly,
　To say it honestly and from the heart,
That we may be allowed to keep lifelong　　　　　　　5
　This lasting pact of sacred friendship.

CX

Aufillena, kind women-friends are always praised:
　They receive reward for what they undertake.
You are no friend, because you broke your promise to me;
　It's criminal to take and never give.
A generous girl gives freely, a modest never promised,　5
　Aufillena; but to rake in gifts
By fraud is theft—worse than the greed of a prostitute
　Whose whole body is up for sale.

CXI

Aufillena, uiro contentam uiuere solo
  nuptarum laus ex laudibus eximiis,
sed cuiuis quamuis potius succumbere par est
  quam matrem fratres ex patruo ⟨parere⟩.

CXII

Multus homo es, Naso, neque tecum multus homo est
    qui
  descendit. Naso, multus es et pathicus.

CXIII

Consule Pompeio primum duo, Cinna,
    solebant
  Maeciliam. facto consule nunc iterum
manserunt duo sed creuerunt milia in
    unum
  singula. fecundum semen adulterio.

CXIV

Firmano saltu non falso Mentula diues
  fertur, qui tot res in se habet egregias—
aucupium omne genus, piscis, prata, arua ferasque.
  nequiquam: fructus sumptibus exsuperat.
quare concedo sit diues dum omnia desint.   5
  saltum laudemus dum modo ipse egeat.

CXV

Mentula habet iuxta triginta iugera prati,
  quadraginta arui; cetera sunt maria.
cur non diuitiis Croesum superare potis sit
  uno qui in saltu tot bona possideat—
prata, arua, ingentes siluas uastasque paludes   5
  usque ad Hyperboreos et mare ad Oceanum?

CXI

That a bride be content, Aufillena, to live with one man
    Is praise among the highest of her praises,
But it's right for any to sleep with anyone she chooses
    Rather than mother cousins by her uncle.

CXII

You're many-sided, Naso, but not many wish to know
    you.
    Naso, you're many-sided—and a poof.

CXIII

In Pompey's first consulship, Cinna, Maecilia was going
    with two.
    Now that he's consul a second time
The two remain but for each there have grown up a
    thousand rivals.
    Adultery propagates fast.

CXIV

TOOL's rightly counted rich in his estate at Firmum,
    For it contains so many excellent things—
Fowl of every kind, fish, pasture, plough, and game.
    But it's no good. He overspends his income.
I grant he's rich, then, if he's short of everything.   5
    Let's praise the estate provided the owner's broke.

CXV

TOOL owns some thirty *iugera* of pasture,
    Forty of ploughland; all the rest is sea.
How can he fail to beat Croesus in riches
    When one estate has so many good things—
Pasture and plough, huge woods and empty marshes   5
    Far as Oceanus' sea and the Hyperboreans?

omnia magna haec sunt, tamen ipse est maximus
    ultro—
  non homo sed uero mentula magna minax.

CXVI

Saepe tibi studioso animo uenante requirens
  carmina uti possem uertere Battiadae,
qui te lenirem nobis neu conarere
  tela infesta meum mittere in usque caput,
hunc uideo mihi nunc frustra sumptum esse laborem,   5
  Gelli, nec nostras hic ualuisse preces.
contra nos tela ista tua euitamus amictu,
  at fixus nostris tu dabi' supplicium.

All these are great things, but their owner's far the
    greatest—
  No human but a great intimidating TOOL.

CXVI

Though often seeking with a studious questing mind
    How to turn for you songs of Battiades
To reconcile you to us and so that you should not keep
    Trying to hurl unfriendly missiles at my head,
I now see that I undertook this task in vain,
    Gellius, and that our pleas were useless here.
Those missiles of yours against us we parry with a cloak,
    But pierced by ours you'll pay the penalty.

EXPLANATORY NOTES

(In I–LX unless otherwise stated the metre is hendecasyllables; see Appendix B 1.)

I

A mock-modest dedication of I–LX to Cornelius Nepos, like Catullus a native of Cisalpine Gaul. Line 6 refers to his lost *Chronica*. Lines 1–2 and 7 indicate, indirectly, that this is poetry in the tradition of Callimachus, the third-century B.C. Alexandrian scholar poet; for *lepidum* is etymologically connected with the Greek word *lepton*, suggesting Callimachus' 'slender' Muse, while 2 and 7 remind one of the hard work and the learning (of metre and of earlier literature) required to compose the sort of poetry approved by Callimachus. *Patrona Virgo* is the Muse. In 10 *saeclo* could also be 'century' or 'age'.

II

A parody of a prayer addressed not to a God but to his girl's pet bird, whose identification with our sparrow is uncertain.

II B

A fragment of another poem, referring to the story of Atalanta. She promised to marry the suitor who could run faster than her, and she was beaten by one who rolled apples of gold in front of her, which she stopped to pick up.

III

Meleager's *Garland* (an anthology of Greek epigrams published around 90 B.C.) contained several epitaphs on dead pets; they can be read in Book VII of the *Greek Anthology*, in particular Nos. 189, 190, 198, 199, 203, 207, and 211. Catullus will have known all these but has here written something very different, with a surprise ending. In 1–2 the connection between *Veneres* and *uenustas* is beyond representation in English.

IV

A technical *tour de force* in pure iambics (see Appendix B 2).
The effect is one of breathless speed. The speaker is usually
taken to be Catullus, speaking for the yacht that brought him
back from Bithynia (see X. 7 and XLVI), and the lake to be
Garda (see XXXI). The yacht is masculine and garrulous; *ait* in
line 2 perhaps represents an inscription on it. The poem
develops from the type of epigram in the *Greek Anthology* in
which an object dedicated to a God speaks. It was well enough
known to be parodied some ten years after Catullus' death in
Catalepton x, attributed to Virgil.

5 and 17 The 'little palms' are oarblades, part of the
personification of the boat.

11 and 13 Cytorus is the modern Kidros, and Amastris
Amasra on the Black Sea.

19–21 It seemed best to render the Latin straight and not to
introduce English nautical terms. The 'feet' are the ropes,
or sheets, at the two lower corners of a square sail.
'Jupiter' here refers to the wind which as Sky-God he
grants.

27 Castor and Pollux (whose name is spondaic and therefore
inadmissible in this metre, but Catullus solves that
problem memorably) were guardian Gods of seafarers.

V

6 *nox* is also used of a night spent with one's love, cf.
English 'date'.

7–9 The regular alternation of 'thousand' and 'hundred'
suggests the moneygrubber steadily increasing his capital.

11–13 *conturbare*: a financial term rather like our 'cooking
the books'. In antiquity 'to count one's blessings was to
invite Nemesis and the evil eye' (Fordyce).

VI

'Catullus pictures himself as peering about his friend Flavius'
bedroom and addressing him there. He notes the bed reeking
with unguents and the worn pillows; he it is who rocks the bed
and makes it creak and dance about' (Munro).

16 *nobis. uolo*: Catullus often uses first person plural for first person singular, sometimes combining the two as here.

VII

basiationes (1) and *lasarpiciferis* (4) are Catullan coinages and presumably polysyllabic humour. The word *basia* itself first occurs in Catullus.

2 Closer: 'were enough and to spare for me, Lesbia'.

4–6 Cyrene was Callimachus' birthplace, and its founder was Battus, from whom he claimed descent (cf. LXV. 16 *Battiades*). Its chief export, silphium, was much used in medicine and cookery. The famous oracle of Jupiter Ammon stood in the oasis of Siwa in the Sahara.

VIII

'Poem VIII gives dramatic form to a struggle in the poet's mind (which the poem records—or rather reconstructs) between intellectual rejection of an impossible situation and emotional reluctance to face the inevitable squarely, and "write off as lost what is plainly lost"' (Quinn).

The self-address comes from drama. The two sides are perhaps at one in *nobis* (5), though see the note on VI. 16.

The metre, scazons or 'limping iambics' (see Appendix B 3), together with the end-stopping of every line, reflects the poet's wavering determination. The translation attempts to represent this feature.

5 Strictly: 'Loved by us as none will be loved'.

IX

The apparent spontaneity of this direct expression of joy contains in the repetition *uenistine . . . uenisti* an allusion to the opening of Theocritus, *Idyll* XII.   Veranius may be the writer on religious antiquities referred to by Festus and Macrobius (Wiseman, 1985, 266–9).

8–9 Such demonstrations of affection were common between friends in the ancient world (cf. Horace, *Satires* I. v. 43 and 93).

X

A conversation piece; with Horace, *Satires* I. ix, one of the very few extant examples of Latin conversation in the Late Republic. Like Horace, Catullus is telling a story against himself.   Varus may be Quintilius Varus, literary critic and friend of Virgil and Horace. Gaius Cinna is the poet of XCV.

22 'heave up . . . head': an attempt to represent *collo . . . collocare*.

27 'To Serapis': i.e. to his temple. He was a popular Egyptian god.

XI

This powerful poem, though clearly later than LI in the same metre, from which it quotes the word *identidem* in the third line of a stanza, is by its position here the first published appearance of sapphics in Latin (see Appendix B 4). In the translation the three sapphic hendecasyllables are each represented by eleven English syllables and the fourth line, or adonic, by five. The poem is dated by lines 10–12 to 55 B.C., the year of Caesar's first invasion of Britain, or early in 54.

1 Furius may be Marcus Furius Bibaculus, a contemporary of Catullus from Cremona, and a poet associated, like Catullus, with Valerius Cato (see LVI). About Aurelius nothing is known.

5–6 Hyrcania lay on the SE side of the Caspian Sea. The Sacae occupied a wide area centring on the modern Tashkent.

7 *septemgeminus*: 'seven-twin', referring to the Nile Delta. *aequora* here may refer to sea or land.

17 *uiue ualeque*: a formula of farewell.

XII

'It is to be remembered that the Romans ate with their fingers (the use of knives and forks is relatively modern) and guests were expected to bring their own table-napkins with them' (Goold).   Asinius Pollio (born in 76 B.C.), friend of Catullus and Cinna, and later of Virgil and Horace, consul in 40 B.C., historian and poet, was an important figure in the literary world of the late Republic.   Saetaban linen was reputedly the finest in Europe (Pliny, *Natural History* XIX. 9).

XIII

A paradoxical development of the conventional poem of invitation, such as Philodemus' to Piso in the *Greek Anthology* xi. 44. Presumably lines 11–12 imply that Lesbia will be there in person.

XIV

This epigram gives us a glimpse of the literary feuds in Catullus' time, though Sulla, Caesius, Aquinus, and Suffenus (apart from XXII) are mere names to us. Gaius Licinius Calvus (famous as an orator for his prosecution of Publius Vatinius, one of Caesar's henchmen—see LIII) wrote epigrams, epithalamia, elegies, and an epyllion, like Catullus (cf. L). Presumably he had sent this anthology as a joke, which Catullus pretends to misunderstand.

XIV B

Wiseman (1969, 7) was the first scholar to see that these lines must have been the beginning of an epigram introducing the group of homosexual epigrams that follows in XV–XXV. Roman tradition was strongly against homosexuality; hence *horrebitis* here.

XV

A paradoxical development of the conventional *commendatio* or letter of recommendation, of which a collection is to be found in Book XIII of Cicero's *Letters to his friends*. Catullus threatens Aurelius with the punishment reserved for adulterers if he makes a pass at his boy-friend. In 16 *nostrum caput* is probably ambiguous, referring to Catullus and to the boy.

XVI

Furius and Aurelius (also paired in XI) clearly hold the traditional view expressed in Buffon's famous remark 'Le style c'est l'homme même'—a view which in fact dates back to the fifth century B.C. On the evidence of Epigram V they have accused Catullus of being effeminate. He pays them back in their own coin, maintaining (the first to do so, as far as we know) that a poet's character is not to be inferred from his work. The epigram is in fact an outspoken defence of the type of poetry Catullus writes.

XVII

The metre is priapeans (see Appendix B 5), capable of brilliant effects, e.g. the rickety bridge (3) or the sticky mud that pulls off the mule's shoe (26). Presumably the Colony (*Colonia*) is Verona, because of 'my fellow townsman' in 8. The word *Salisubsalus* is found nowhere else; it is probably a cult title of Mars, whose priests were known as *Salii* or Jumpers.

XXI

This follows XVII in the MSS; for the gap in the numbering see Introduction, p. xi. Here Aurelius is characterized (or more probably libelled) not as some kind of dieting health-freak, though there were such in ancient Rome too, but as a mere *scurra* or parasite, who lives by sponging on rich patrons and is seldom sure where his next meal is coming from. His title in line 1 probably means 'Chief of all the hungry'.

13 *finem facias*: perhaps 'achieve your aim' as well as 'end up'.

XXII

Re-enter Varus (from X) and Suffenus (from XIV). This epigram in scazons gives us a further insight into the sort of poetry Catullus and his friends approve, and implies the attitude they think the poet should have to his work. The last four lines are surprisingly unlike the Catullus we have got to know so far and very Horatian in their humanity, cf. Horace, *Satires* i. i. 69–70 *mutato nomine de te/fabula narratur*, 'change the name and the story's about you'. *Probe* in line 1 is possibly a *double entendre*, as at Terence, *Adelphi* 753.

XXIII

An ironical *makarismos* or poem of congratulation, with a surprise ending. Furius should learn to count his blessings.

XXIV

The Juventii were an aristocratic Roman clan of Etruscan origin; the name also occurs in inscriptions of Imperial date in the Verona area (Neudling, 94). By naming his boy-friend here Catullus is flouting convention, the more so because from line 5 the reader can deduce that this anonymous lover is the penniless Furius.

XXV

An epigram like XII, but remarkable for its liberal use of diminutives, alliteration, and assonance, and written in a rare metre for Catullus—catalectic iambic tetrameters (see Appendix B 6). Thallos is a Greek name.

   5 Text uncertain. 'The Goddess of hawks' would be Laverna, Goddess of thieves. The hawk metaphor is kept up in *inuolasti* (6) and *unguibus* (9).

XXVI

The point of this epigram is the pun on *opposita* 'facing' and 'mortgaged', and the subsidiary one on *uentum* 'wind' and 'luck', cf. Cicero, *Letters to Atticus* II. i. 6 (*Caesaris*) *nunc uenti ualde sunt secundi*, 'Caesar's winds are now very favourable'.

XXVII

It was not until 1969 that the purpose of this epigram was understood—by Wiseman (1969, 7–8). Ostensibly it is a *skolion* or drinking song, but its real subject is poetry; *calices amariores* refers to the invectives against Piso, Memmius, Mamurra, Pompey, Caesar, and other powerful public figures that follow. So far Catullus has only attacked by name members of his private circle. Here there is an attack on Postumia, who may be the wife of the famous lawyer Servius

Sulpicius Rufus and the rumoured mistress of Caesar. Line 3 would then be a witty reference to the phrase *imperia Postumiana*, which arose from the fifth-century dictator, Postumius Tubertus, ordering the execution of his own son (see Cairns, 1975, 27–8). *Thyonianus* is a cult title of Bacchus derived from the Greek *thuein* 'to rage'.

XXVIII

Veranius and Fabullus were last heard of in Spain (XII. 14–16), but there is no record of a Piso as governor there. This Piso is usually identified with Caesar's father-in-law Lucius Calpurnius Piso Caesoninus, proconsul in Macedonia 57–55 B.C. (see Wiseman, 1969, 38–40). Memmius has already appeared anonymously at X. 13 and is here attacked openly. Catullus and his friends are of opinion that the Roman Empire should be run for their personal enrichment.

6–8 Difficult. Most take *expensum* with line 6, translating with Goold: 'Do profits show in your account-books/on the wrong side, as with me, who in service with/my governor reckon my outgoings as profit?' Scaliger, understanding *refero datum lucello* as 'I record as entered on the credit side', took lines 9–10 as the actual entry.

XXIX

Iambi against Mamurra, Caesar's chief engineer, Pompey (*cinaede Romule*), and Caesar himself (*imperator unice*). Mamurra served under Pompey in the war against Mithridates (hence 18 *praeda Pontica*) and thereafter with Caesar in Spain, Gaul, and Britain. Pompey married Caesar's daughter Julia; hence 24 *socer generque*. Metre: pure iambics, broken in the first foot of line 3 to accommodate the proper name. Textual trouble in 20 and 23. Date: probably late 55 B.C. in the consulship of Pompey and Crassus and after Caesar's first invasion of Britain.

3–4 *Comata Gallia*: Transalpine Gaul, NW of the Alps.

21 Or, taking *malum* with *hunc*, 'this crook'.

XXX

An attack on a false friend, whose identity is uncertain, in greater asclepiads, a metre difficult to manage in Latin (see

Appendix B 7). 'Alfenus had led him unsuspecting into love—with whom? . . . He doesn't tell us so there is no point in asking. What he does tell us is that honest dealing is required in the investment of emotional capital; the gods of good faith do not approve of those who lead you on and then cynically back out of the deal. Poem 30 is a very revealing document, but too uncomfortably self-pitying to be an artistic success. Catullus was not usually so nakedly vulnerable' (Wiseman, 1985, 123).

This is the first appearance in Catullus of the idea of *Fides*, so important to his view of life. Compare, from Ariadne's lament in LXIV, 132 *perfide*, 134 *neglecto numine Diuum*, 135 *immemor*, 142 *aerii . . . irrita uenti*.

XXXI

Metre: scazons. Date: 56 B.C. (cf. XLVI). Sirmio, Catullus' family home on Lake Garda, is personified and greeted as a beautiful slave-girl. There are touches of Alexandrian learning: Neptune is God of fresh as well as salt water; Thynia is the land of the Thyni, who occupy the coastal region of Bithynia; the waves are Lydian because the Etruscans (who had settlements in the Po valley) were believed to have come from Lydia in Asia Minor. There is a full discussion of this poem by Cairns (1974).

XXXII

'These elegant, outrageous *uersiculi* are hardly a historical document which has come into our hands by accident. Plainly Ipsitilla, if she existed, is being got at' (Quinn, 1970).

1 *Amabo*, 'I will love', is also used in Latin for 'please'.
   Ipsitilla, if that is what Catullus wrote, may be a diminutive of *ipsa*—'dear little mistress'.

8 *fututiones*: a nonce word, borrowed later by Martial.

XXXIII

Nothing more is known about Vibennius and Son. The theft of clothing from the public baths was common in antiquity.

XXXIV

The position of this fine hymn is no doubt intended to surprise, if not to shock, the reader. It may have been written for musical performance on a special occasion—at the annual festival of Diana on the Aventine in Rome (Bentley, *Horace*, praefatio) or of Apollo on Delos, 'a centre for the transmission of corn supplies to Rome' (Wiseman, 1985, 96–9). For the metre see Appendix B 8.

  21–2 It is important to address the Goddess by her right name; this formula covers all omissions.

XXXV

A Caecilius is mentioned at LXVII. 9, though at Verona, not Como (where the name is common in inscriptions. Both Plinys were Caecilii from Como).   For *Dindymi Dominam* see LXIII. 91. So Caecilius' poem on Cybele, the Great Mother, may have been in galliambics, like LXIII, or an epyllion in dactylic hexameters, like LXIV. In either case, according to Catullus, it was by no means finished; it needed more work.

XXXVI

Volusius' *Annals*, attacked again at XCV. 7, will have been an historical epic in the tradition of Ennius' *Annales*, a tradition from which Catullus and his friends were anxious to escape.

  5 One should probably understand 'at her', *sibi* (4) doing double duty.

  7 'the Hobble-footed God' is Vulcan.

  12–15 The places here mentioned were mostly cult-centres of Venus.

XXXVII

This lampoon in scazons looks back to VIII and the penultimate stanza of XI and is an example of the *iambi* referred to in XXXVI. The *salax taberna* could be Clodia's grand house on the Palatine near the temple of Castor and Pollux, who were often depicted as wearing caps like egg-cosies. Egnatius may be the poet who wrote a *De Rerum Natura* from which Macrobius quotes two fragments.

XXXVIII and XXXIX

Both (the second in scazons) presumably arise out of the situation represented in XXXVII. Cornificius was a poet of whose work there has survived one hendecasyllabic line, together with part of a hexameter from his epyllion entitled *Glaucus*. Simonides of Ceos flourished around 500 B.C. and was famous for his *Threnoi* or 'Dirges'.

XL

It seems natural to regard Ravidus too (scanned here as a disyllable, *Raude*) as one of the *semitarii moechi* of XXXVII, like Egnatius. The opening is reminiscent of one of Archilochus' *iambi*:

> Father Lycambes, what is this you said?
> Who led your wits astray
> Which earlier were fixed? But now you cause
> The citizens much mirth.
>
> Fragment 172 (West)

and so, like the opening of IX, it provides another example of Catullus' *doctrina*.

> 5–6 Literally: 'Is it so you may reach the mouths of the mob?/What do you want? Do you choose to be known no matter how?'

XLI

Here we return to Mamurra (XXIX above), 'the bankrupt from Formiae', and meet his girl-friend. *aes*, 'bronze', was used for mirrors as well as money.

XLII

In the small communities of ancient Italy a man who had suffered an injustice would round up his friends, and together they would go to the house of the man who had wronged him. There, loudly and with insults, they would demand redress.

The custom was known as *flagitatio*, and Catullus assumes knowledge of it here. The woman in question is an adulteress and therefore (on the evidence so far available to the reader) Lesbia herself (cf. XI. 17 *moechis*, XXXVII. 16 *moechi*).

5 *pugillaria* and *codicilli* 'were wax-coated wooden writing-tablets, with a rim to prevent rubbing, hinged together in pairs or sets by straps at one side, and used for writing which was not meant to be permanent' (Fordyce).

24 Literally: 'Moral and modest, give back the notebook'.

XLIII

A meeting with Mamurra's mistress as line 5 shows (cf. XLI. 4). 'The Province' is Cisalpine Gaul, Catullus' own *patria*. Presumably we have here a negative picture of Lesbia.

XLIV

A parody in scazons of a *soterion* or thank-offering to a God for deliverance. Tibur (Tivoli) was more fashionable than the Sabine hills. Sestius was tribune in 57 B.C. and helped recall Cicero from exile. Nothing more is known of his speech against Antius, but Cicero agrees with Catullus about his prose; referring to an example of it he writes to Atticus 'I have never read anything more *Sestiodious*' (*Letters to Atticus* VII. xvii. 2).

XLV

Line 22 probably dates this famous love-duet to 55 B.C. when Caesar and Crassus were planning their expeditions against Britain and Syria respectively, and ambitious young Romans were rushing to join up in the hope of riches. Acme would be a Greek freedwoman (the name occurs in Republican inscriptions). Ferguson sees this poem as a 'companion-piece' to XI, written in the same year.

26 Literally: 'Who a better-omened Venus?'

XLVI

For the dating of this poem see Introduction, p. xviii. Book x of the *Greek Anthology* opens with several epigrams greeting the return of spring, some of which Catullus will have known. What he does here, *inter alia*, is to personalize a topic of Greek epigram. Nicaea was capital of the Roman province of Bithynia.

XLVII

A sequel to XXVIII. Porcius may have been C. Porcius Cato, a Caesarian and tribune in 56 B.C.; Socration ('Pocket Socrates') is perhaps a nickname for the Epicurean scholar-poet Philodemus, a protégé of Lucius Calpurnius Piso Caesoninus.

2 The implication of *sinistrae* (cf. XII. 1) is that they practised extortion in the province on Piso's behalf. From 5–6 we gather that they had their rake-off.

6 *de die*: to dine before the end of the working day was considered Sybaritic.

XLVIII

A companion piece to V and VII. *aridus* and *arista* were thought to be etymologically connected.

XLIX

Probably ironical because of the correlation in the last two lines. Catullus does not really think he is 'the worst poet of all', so it follows that he doesn't really think Cicero 'the best advocate of all', though as Goold puts it he may be 'the best advocate-of-all', i.e. 'the greatest unprincipled advocate'. Cicero attacked Vatinius in 56 B.C. and defended him two years later, when Catullus' friend Calvus was prosecuting. The position of this epigram supports the connection with Vatinius, who is mentioned in LII and LIII.

L

For this epigram see Introduction, p. xxiii.

LI

Generally taken to be the first poem that Catullus wrote to Clodia, just as XI in the same metre is taken to be the last. The first three stanzas are a translation in the same metre (sapphics) of Sappho, Fragment 31. Catullus adds line 2, the words *identidem*, *spectat et*, *misero*, the name *Lesbia*, and the final stanza, where *otium* could also be translated 'idleness'.

LII

A lampoon on two supporters of the Triumvirate of Pompey, Caesar, and Crassus. 'The juxtaposition with Poem LI is pointed. Lesbia confers divinity; Vatinius and Nonius make mortality welcome' (Ferguson). Metre: iambic trimeters.

Nonius is probably Marcus Nonius Sufenas who was tribune in 56 B.C. and could have been curule aedile in 54. Vatinius was not consul until 47 B.C., but he was praetor in 55 and could have thought the consulship was in his pocket.

LIII

Probably refers to Calvus' prosecution of Vatinius in 54 B.C. Quintilian reports that some people thought Calvus a finer orator than Cicero. Seneca the Elder has a story that Vatinius interrupted Calvus to say to the jury 'Am I to be found guilty because this man is articulate?' The meaning of *salaputium* is uncertain, but it must have had something to do with Calvus' short stature. *Caluos* is the earlier spelling of Caluus (cf. LXI. 54).

LIV

For text and interpretation of this obscure attack on supporters of Caesar see Munro, 122–9.

LV

This mysterious epigram (with textual trouble in 9 and 11) is on a similar theme to VI, except that here the lover himself cannot be found and on the evidence of 13–14 and 22 the poet is in love with him. The reference to Pompey's Portico (6) dates it to 55 B.C. or later. The metre is experimental, mixing decasyllables containing a spondee as third and fourth syllables in the line with hendecasyllables.

2 'hide-out': literally 'darkness'.

12 This would make some sense if with Frank Copley we suppose that the name Camerius suggests some Greek word for brassière.

LVI

The 'pay-off' here (such as it is) is surely weakened by the overblown introduction. The translation of 5–7 is based on Housman's interpretation; *cecidi* is a pun on flogging and sexual intercourse. Cato is probably the poet and critic Publius Valerius Cato, summed up in the anonymous fragment

> *Cato grammaticus, Latina Siren,*
> *qui solus legit ac facit poetas*
>
> Grammarian Cato, Latin Siren,
> Who alone reads and creates poets.

He would at least appreciate that the opening alludes to Archilochus, Fragment 168 (West):

> Erasmonides Charilaos, I'll tell you a funny thing,
> And, far dearest of comrades, you'll enjoy listening.

LVII

Like XXIX a direct attack on Caesar and his chief engineer, but even more scabrous.

3–5 A reference to the bankruptcy of both.

6 'didymous': Ernst Schmidt explains this as a reference to their double nature sexually; 'diseased' because pathic.

7 Apart from his *Commentaries* Caesar wrote a grammatical monograph *De Analogia* and poetry. Mamurra too wrote poetry (see CV) and may be identical with Vitruvius, the writer on architecture.

8 *uorax*: cf. XXIX. 2.

LVIII

Usually taken as addressed to Marcus Caelius Rufus, a brilliant young protégé of Cicero, who supplanted Catullus as Clodia's lover; hence *Lesbia nostra* here. But see Introduction, p. xxi. This invective resembles LIX and LX in consisting of a single sentence of five lines.

LVIII B

Continues the experimental metre of LV. Camerius is still unobtainable and the message is that Catullus has lost interest in him.

1 Talos, a huge bronze robot made for Minos of Crete by the Fire-God Hephaistos; he ran round Crete three times a day.

2 *Ladas*: a famous Spartan long-distance runner.   Perseus was lent winged sandals by the Nymphs for his fight against the Gorgon Medusa.

3 The winged horse Pegasus sprang up from Medusa's blood when Perseus beheaded her.

4 Rhesus was the Thracian king whose wind-swift horses were stolen by Ulysses.

LIX

'The first line has a kind of lapidary, or rather graffital, finality' (Quinn, 1969). The reader knows nothing about the reason behind this bitter attack or about the persons mentioned. Metre: scazons, regularly used for invective.

LX

Scazons again, in the high style contrasting with the low style of LIX. An epigram on the theme of betrayal (cf. XXX), remarkably like Ariadne's words at LXIV. 154–7. 'The emphasis on Scylla's barking groin is not a commonplace, however: after Poems LVIII and LIX, and in the metre of invective, it reminds us of sex and shamelessness' (Wiseman, 1985, 157). The reader naturally takes 'you' as Lesbia and the 'suppliant' as Catullus, though 'his' is not in the Latin of line 4.

LXI

A dramatic choral ode in Greek style and metre (see Appendix B 8) celebrating and describing a real Roman wedding between Junia (if that is her name at line 16) Aurunculeia (82–3) and Manlius Torquatus (16 and 209). Torquatus is usually taken to be the scholar and orator who defends Epicureanism in

Cicero's dialogue *De Finibus*. The poet acts as *choregus* or chorus leader directing and commenting on the course of events throughout.

2 Helicon: a mountain in Boeotia, home of the nine Muses.

Urania: the Heavenly One, mother of Hymen the God of marriage according to Callimachus, and Muse of astronomy.

8 The *flammeum* was a veil covering the Roman bride from head to foot.

18–19 A reference to the famous Judgement of Paris between the three Goddesses, Juno, Minerva, and Venus.

27–30 *Thespiae*: a Boeotian (Aonian) town below Helicon.

Aganippe: the Muses' spring, also Hippocrene.

54 *nouos*: the old spelling of *nouus*, cf. LIII. 3 *Caluos*.

119 Ancient etymology links Fescennine with *fascinum* 'phallus'. The ribaldry is designed to avoid the jealousy of the Gods by cutting fortunate human beings down to size.

127 Talassius: the Roman marriage-God.

129 *uilicae*: 'bailiffs' wives'.

175 The *praetexta* was a toga bordered with purple worn by free-born Roman children.

221 Penelope: Ulysses' wife, faithful to him for the twenty years of his absence from Ithaca.

LXII

Another dramatic choral poem, this time enacting a contest between a choir of young men and a choir of girls at an imaginary wedding-feast, in dactylic hexameters (see Appendix B 9) and with one or two allusions to Sappho. At the same time 'the legalistic Roman attitude to marriage is spelt out with disconcerting clarity: what matters is the contract between the bride's parents and the groom, and the bride's virginity is an asset in which she herself holds only a minority share' (Wiseman, 1985, 111).

1 *Vesper*: here Hesperus, the Evening Star.

2 Or 'from Olympus', if the word is here used of the sky.

7 Mt. Oeta in Thessaly was associated in Greek poetry with Hesperus.

32 The girls begin their stanza, but the rest of it, plus refrain, has dropped out. From 33 to 38 we are back with the boys.

58 The MSS give no refrain after this line. According to Fraenkel, the boys, knowing that they have won, at 59 turn at once to the bride.

LXIII

A powerful narrative poem in galliambics (see Appendix B 10), the only complete ancient example of that metre, which was confined to poems about Cybele. It has a Greek background, as is shown by the Greek nouns in line 60, *ephebus* (63), compound adjectives such as *hederigerae* (23), *properipedem* (34), *erifugae* (51), the reference to Pasithea (43), and of course the story itself. The worship of Cybele, the Great Mother, had been brought to Rome early in the third century B.C., when she was given a temple on the Palatine. Her eunuch priests were called Galli, after the river Gallus in Phrygia, the birthplace and centre of her cult. Catullus chooses to use the feminine *Gallae*.

13 Dindymus: a mountain in Phrygia.

43 In *Iliad* XIV Hypnos, God of sleep, wins his wife Pasithea (one of the Graces) as a reward from Hera for putting Zeus to sleep.

LXIV

Presumably Catullus would have regarded this epyllion as his masterpiece and hoped that it might stand comparison with Cinna's *Zmyrna* (whose publication he greets in XCV), Calvus' *Io*, and Cornificius' *Glaucus* (two lost epyllia that we hear about from other sources). Its main characteristic is a studied avoidance of the obvious, the straightforward, and the expected. It differs from the epyllia mentioned above in not dealing with a story in any way bizarre or perverted, and in not containing a metamorphosis of the main character. We do not know what title Catullus gave it, but it is usually referred to as *The Marriage of Peleus and Thetis* because that is the story dealt with in lines 1–49 and 267–383. The coverlet on the marriage-bed enables Catullus to inset the story of Theseus, Bacchus, and Ariadne (50–266). Surprisingly this inner theme is dealt with at much greater length than the outer one, occupying 217 lines as against 166. The poem ends with an epilogue of 25 lines contrasting the Heroic Age with the poet's own day. The method of narration is equally surprising. Narrative proper is reduced to a minimum. The poet selects certain key moments for special treatment, e.g. how Peleus fell in love with Thetis, Ariadne deserted on the shore, her dramatic monologue, Aegeus' farewell speech to his son Theseus, the arrival of Bacchus and his revellers, a description of the Parcae spinning, their wedding-song foretelling the birth and prowess of Achilles.

Every line of the poem is most carefully considered and will often be found to contain a miniature point or notable feature: 1–2 *prognatae* and *nasse* applied to trees; 3 the chiastic arrangement with the spondaic adjectival ending answering the genitive noun at the beginning; 4 the phrase *robora pubis*; 5 'gilded hide' referring to the famous Golden Fleece; 7 *palmis* used of oars. The reader is also expected to pick up allusions, e.g. to Ennius' *Medea* and Apollonius' *Argonautica* at the beginning, and to know, say, that Prometheus (294–7) was freed from his chains when he told Zeus the secret that Thetis was fated to bear a son greater than his father, or that Apollo and his sister did not attend the wedding (299–302) because Apollo would later kill its offspring Achilles, and probably too that Theseus was *immemor* 'heedless, forgetful' (58) because Bacchus, in love with Ariadne himself, caused him to forget about her. Nevertheless it is perfectly possible to enjoy the poem without such knowledge, just as one can enjoy, say, Eliot's *Waste Land* without recognizing any of its numerous allusions.

1–10 The Argo, first ocean-going ship as opposed to coaster, carried the Argonauts in quest of the Golden Fleece to the river Phasis in Colchis (Georgia), the realm of king Aeetes.

8 The Goddess Athena.

11 Amphitrite, wife of Neptune, represents the open sea.

21 *Pater ipse*: Jupiter, who had wished to marry Thetis himself, until he learnt from Prometheus that her son was destined to be greater than his father.

29 *Tethys*: wife of Oceanus.

35–7 Thessalian place-names.

52 Dia was the old name for Naxos in the Cyclades (Callimachus, Fragment 601).

60 *Minois*: Minos' daughter.

72 *Erycina*: because Venus had a famous temple on Mt. Eryx in NW Sicily.

75 *Gortynia*: the adjective must be used here (by the figure of speech known as synecdoche or part for whole) for 'Cretan', for the Labyrinth was at Cnossos in the North of Crete, whereas Gortyn was some 16 kms from the South coast.

77 Androgeos, Minos' son, was killed on a visit to Athens after competing successfully in the Panathenaic Games. Minos held Aegeus, king of Athens and Theseus' father, responsible and in compensation demanded an annual tribute of seven young Athenians of both sexes.

79 *Cecropiam*: Athens, because founded by Cecrops.

   Minotauro: the Minotaur, a monster with the head of a bull and the body of a man, fed on human flesh and was hidden away in the Labyrinth in Crete.

89 Eurotas: a river in Sparta.

95–6 refer to Cupid and Venus; Golgi and Idalium were cult-centres of hers in Cyprus.

105 Taurus: a mountain range in Cilicia, presumably chosen because of the verbal connection with *Minotaurus*.

113 Ariadne had given Theseus a ball of thread to unwind as he went into the Labyrinth, so that he could find his way out again.

141 Goold notes that the hexameter can also be regarded as a combination of glyconic and pherecratean, the metre used for wedding songs (cf. LXI):

> *sed conubia laeta, sed*
> *optatos hymenaeos.*

178 Mt. Ida in Crete.

211 Erechtheus was Aegeus' ancestor, and his port the Piraeus.

212 Athena, referred to in 228 as *Incola Itoni* because she had a famous temple there.

217 Theseus was brought up by his mother and met his father for the first time on reaching manhood.

227 A dye from Spain.

251 *Iacchus*: a cult name of Bacchus.

252 The Sileni or elder Satyrs came from Nysa, a legendary place where Bacchus was born and they brought him up.

253 After this line Mynors supposes a lacuna.

259 *orgia*: secret holy objects.

279 *Chiron*: the wise Centaur, later to become Achilles' tutor.

282 Favonius was the Latin equivalent of Zephyros, the west wind.

283 Or, reading *in distinctis*, 'in assorted bunches'.

285 *Penios*: a Thessalian river-god.

287 Text uncertain. Haemonia was another name for Thessaly.

290–1 After Phaethon fell to his death while driving the chariot of the Sun, his weeping sisters were turned into poplars.

300 A cryptic reference to Apollo's sister Diana. *unigena* ought to mean 'only begotten', but at LXVI. 53 Catullus uses it to translate the Greek word *gnotos* 'sibling'.

306 *Parcae*: literally 'the Sparing Ones', the Latin equivalent of the Greek Moirai or Fates.

324 Emathia: strictly Macedonia, but used here by metonymy for Thessaly.   Ops: Saturn's wife and Jupiter's mother. 'Housman's repunctuation of this line on which, in the form *Emathiae tutamen opis*, *carissime* (or *clarissime*) *nato*, editors had exercised their ingenuity for centuries, is the most spectacular contribution of modern scholarship to the interpretation of Catullus' (Fordyce).

326 In fact the antecedent of *quae* is not *fusi* but *subtegmina*: 'But run, you spindles, drawing out the weft which the fates follow.'

344 Teucer was the first king of Troy; hence the Trojans were called *Teucri* 'Teucers, Teucrians'.

346 A reference to Agamemnon, leader of the Greeks in the Trojan War.

355 *infesto*: for the translation 'raised' see *Oxford Latin Dictionary* s.v. 3 c.

357 Scamander: a river in the Troad.

367 The walls of Troy had been built by Neptune.

368 Polyxena was a daughter of King Priam and his wife Hecuba.

376–7 It was an ancient belief that the loss of virginity thickened the neck.

378 This line in the MSS repeats the refrain inappropriately and is omitted by editors.

390 *Liber*: an Italian vegetation God identified with the Greek Bacchus.

394 *Mauors*: an older form of Mars, the God of war.

395 *Tritonis Era*: Athena, born beside the legendary river Triton.

    Amarynthia Virgo: Artemis/Diana who had a cult-centre at Amarynthus in Euboea.

402 Text uncertain.

406 *iustificam*: literally 'just-making, justifying'. The adjective occurs here only.

LXV

A covering letter in elegiac couplets (see Appendix B 11), sending LXVI (a translation from Callimachus) to Quintus Hortensius Hortalus, Cicero's oratorical rival, who had apparently asked Catullus for a poem, and who himself wrote love poems and an historical epic (see XCV). Catullus handles his couplets in the Greek manner, allowing polysyllabic endings to the pentameter and constructing the poem as one long sentence, whose protasis beginning *Etsi* is answered by an apodosis beginning *sed tamen* (15). Both parts of this long sentence end with a simile. The tone and content of the final simile are designed to lead into the mood of the following translation.

7 Rhoeteum: a promontory in the Troad.

13–14 *Daulias*: the nightingale, a princess of Daulis turned into a bird for the murder of her son Itylus.

16 *Battiadae*: see note on VII. 6.

23 Literally: '. . . is carried headlong by its downward rush'. The bumping is mostly suggested by the rhythm of the line.

LXVI

In 247 B.C. Ptolemy III (Euergetes), on ascending the throne of Egypt, married his second cousin Berenice, daughter of the king of Cyrene, and then went off to fight a war in Syria. Berenice vowed a lock of her hair for his safe return and duly dedicated it in the Pantheon at Alexandria when he returned victorious. But the lock of hair disappeared from the temple. The disappearance, however, enabled Conon, the astronomer royal, to claim that the constellation he had recently discovered between Virgo and the Great Bear was in fact Berenice's lock, instarred as Ariadne's crown had been. To celebrate the metamorphosis Callimachus wrote a poem in elegiac couplets which he later included in his *Aitia*. Of this poem some thirty lines have survived on papyrus, and comparison of them with Catullus' Latin version in the same metre shows that he keeps as close to the Greek as he can. We may guess that he chose to translate this particular example of Alexandrian court poetry partly as a technical exercise, but mainly because of its concern with love, separation, and marriage, the themes of LXI–LXIV and LXVII–LXVIII, not to mention many of the epigrams.

5–6 A reference to the story of Endymion, the shepherd on Mt. Latmos in Caria, with whom the Moon-Goddess Diana fell in love; she visited him during the dark times between the old moon and the new. For Diana as Trivia see XXXIV. 15.

22 The king and queen of Egypt were regarded not only as husband and wife but as brother and sister, like Zeus and Hera (Jupiter and Juno).

27–8 Berenice's father had betrothed her to Ptolemy Euergetes, but on her father's death her mother arranged for her to marry a cousin of Ptolemy's. This cousin, however, became the mother's lover, and Berenice procured his assassination.

44 *progenies Thiae*: Boreas the north wind. Thia was wife of Hyperion the Sun-God and grandmother of the four winds.

45–6 During his invasion of Greece the Persian king Xerxes cut a canal in 483 B.C. through the isthmus of Mt. Athos in Chalcidice.

47 Literally 'What will hair do when such things yield to iron?'

48 The Chalybes, reputedly the first iron-workers, were a tribe inland from Trebizond on the Black Sea.

50 *stringere*: both 'unsheathe' and 'case-harden'.

52 Zephyrus the west wind, like black Memnon, was a son of Eos/Aurora, the Dawn (daughter of Thia—see 44 note).

54–6 Arsinoe, wife of Ptolemy II, was deified after her death and given a temple at Zephyrium near Canopus as Aphrodite (Venus) Zephyritis; so naturally she chose Zephyrus as messenger.

66 *Callisto*: the Great Bear.

70 Tethys is Oceanus' wife (cf. LXIV. 29).

71 *Ramnusia Virgo*: Nemesis, the Goddess who punishes human arrogance, had a famous temple at Rhamnus in Attica.

92–3 Text disputed. Mynors gives: '. . . treat me to much largesse./If only the stars would fall down! Let me become a royal lock.'

LXVII

We have just listened to a dramatic monologue spoken by Berenice's Lock; now we hear an enigmatic dialogue between the poet and the Door of a house in Verona which is at present occupied by the poet's friend Caecilius (see XXXV). The poet hints at scandal about the wife of the house's previous occupant. The Door explains that she had been married before in Brixia (Brescia) and had behaved badly there too.

5–8 So Balbus Senior was a widower and the Door, when Balbus Junior marries, symbolizes the new wife. She was unfaithful, so the Door can be accused of grudging service and disloyalty.

31–4 So what we have just been told in 19–28 took place in Brixia.

Cycneae . . . speculae (if that adjective is the right reading) presumably refers to a hill named after Cycnus, who was turned into a swan (*cycnus*) while mourning the death of his friend Phaethon.

35 'A large number of inscriptions from Brixia belongs to the gens Postumia' (Neudling).   Cornelius is unlikely to be Cornelius Nepos (see I), who probably came from Ticinum (Pavia), but may be the Cornelius of CII.

LXVIII A

Manlius (presumably the aristocratic Manlius Torquatus whose marriage LXI celebrates) is having trouble with his love-life; he cannot sleep nor can he find pleasure in classical Greek poetry as he lies awake. So he asks Catullus 'for gifts both of the Muses and of Venus', a phrase which is most naturally taken as meaning for poetry and for some form of sexual consolation (precisely what is not explained). Catullus gives reasons for refusing both requests: first his brother's death has so shattered him that he now has no desire for love affairs (or to compose poetry?); secondly, he has few authors (33—or writings?) with him as his library is at his base in Rome. At this point, without further apology, the letter ends.

10 Some scholars interpret as 'learned love poetry', but this does not square with two requests; others think that Manlius is asking Catullus to provide him with a girl, others that he is propositioning Catullus himself.

15 *uestis . . . pura*: the plain white *toga uirilis* or toga of manhood assumed by boys about the age of 16.

28–9 Another crux. Goold translates 'at Verona, where everyone of the upper class has / to warm his cold limbs in an empty bed', and notes that 'Manlius (who wrote from Rome) is insisting that in Verona Catullus like other young aristocrats could not engage in amorous pursuits with the same freedom possible in the capital'. I have adopted Camps's version, who takes the lines as referring to a particular affair of Lesbia's, perhaps the one with Caelius.

33–6 Usually taken as implying that in order to compose learned poetry he needs his library; in other words *scriptorum* does not refer to 'writings' of his own but to 'writers'.

LXVIII B

Catullus changes his mind and does after all write a poem for Manlius in gratitude for his providing a house where Catullus and his mistress—his 'radiant goddess' (70), who is also an adulteress (145–6) and has other lovers (135–6), therefore presumably Lesbia—could meet and make love. But in this poem he refers to Manlius as Allius in order to conceal his identity and to avoid public scandal (though in fact *me Allius* (41) when spoken would sound very like *Mallius*, the ordinary pronunciation of the name spelt *Manlius*). Catullus' poetical thank-offering is of uniquely intricate construction, even more complicated than LXIV. Like LXIV it has an inset into the main theme, viz. the simile about Laodamia and Protesilaus which, with its own attendant similes and digressions, extends from 73 to 130—for 58 out of 120 lines. This inset is itself most curiously constructed. One may represent its contents very roughly thus: Laodamia (73–86), Troy (87–90), Catullus' brother's death (91–8, lines more or less repeating LXVIII A 19–24), Troy (99–104), Laodamia (105–30). It is remarkable that similes occupy no less than 64 of the 120 lines of LXVIII B. In gratitude to Manlius (the more lively and sincere because of the initial refusal in LXVIII A) Catullus offers him a most original example of learned love poetry.

51 *Amathusia*: Venus, cf. XXXVI. 14.

53 *Trinacria rupes*: Etna, Sicily being 'the three-cornered island'.

54 The pass of Thermopylae (Hot Gates) on Mt. Oeta in Malis was named after the hot springs there.

65 See note on IV. 27.

68 'me and my mistress': literally 'us and the mistress', cf. 156.

72 'with creaking sandal': or 'tapping with her sandal'.

74 The details of the story of Laodamia and Protesilaus are not known and what lines 75–6 refer to remains a mystery. Protesilaus was the first of the Greeks to land and die at Troy, having had only one day with Laodamia after their marriage.

77 *Ramnusia Virgo*: Nemesis, cf. note on LXVI. 71.

109–16 Underground channels near the town of Pheneus, draining the plain below Mt. Cyllene in Arcadia, were believed to have been dug by Hercules (supposedly Amphitryon's son but really Jupiter's) when he had killed the man-eating birds of Lake Stymphalus on the orders of Eurystheus, 'his inferior lord'. After his death on the pyre on Mt. Oeta Hercules ascended into heaven and there married Hebe, the Goddess of Youth.

133 So Lesbia was an epiphany of Venus. For the saffron tunic cf. note on LXI. 8.

142 Cf. LXXII. 3–4.

147 'I alone': the Latin has 'we alone'.

153 *Themis*: the Greek Goddess of Justice.

156 'I and my mistress': literally 'we and the mistress', cf. 68.

157 The last three words of the Latin line are quite uncertain. Scaliger's *te tradidit*, though better than nothing, is unlikely to be right, because Manlius was the aristocrat and the lower in status should be introduced to the higher.

LXIX

Rufus (the name re-appears in LXXVII and Rufulus in LIX) has generally been thought to be Caelius Rufus (see note on LVIII).

LXX

Behind this personal epigram stands an impersonal one by Callimachus:

Swore Callignotus to Ionis he would never
  Hold boy or girl dearer than her.
He swore, but the saying's true that the ears of the immortals
  Are deaf to lovers' promises.
So now his flame is male, but of the wretched girl,
  Like Megara, 'no word or reckoning'.

LXXI

The reading *apte* in line 4 is not certain and may conceal the name of an addressee to whom *tuus* could refer. As it is, we may perhaps suppose Catullus to be talking to himself—about the Rufus of LXIX.

LXXII

A development of LXX. 'He tries to fix in words the peculiarity of his feeling for Lesbia and to give expression to a way of feeling that was new for antiquity' (Kroll).

2 *uelle*: should perhaps be taken with *nosse* (1) as well as with *tenere*—'that you only wanted to know Catullus and would refuse to embrace . . .'

7 *iniuria*: 'injury' or 'injustice' might be better than 'hurt'.

8 *bene uelle*: used of the feeling between friends.

LXXIII

Like XXX, on the theme of friendship betrayed. The last line with its five elisions has been criticized as clumsy; but the fact is that Catullus uses elision to express strong emotion, cf. LXVIII. 89–90 (D. A. West. 'The Metre of Catullus' Elegiacs', *Classical Quarterly* NS 7 (1957), 98–102). The friend is probably the Rufus of LXXVII or maybe Gellius (see XCI).

LXXIV

Gellius gets more stick later on. He is reckoned to be Lucius Gellius Poplicola, son of the consul of 72 B.C. and a friend of Clodius; the charge of incest is supported by Valerius Maximus. Uncles (or, to be precise, father's brothers, *patrui*) were proverbial as guardians of morality.

4 Harpocrates, or the Child Horus, son of the Egyptian Goddess Isis, is represented in art as a chubby infant with his left forefinger to his lips.

LXXV

A compressed re-working of the antithesis at the end of LXXII.

LXXVI

A complex and powerful poem which lacks the immediate lyrical appeal of VIII but whose doggedly prosaic style in the end makes an even stronger impression on the reader.

2 *pium*: *pius* and *pietas* are hard words to translate. The man who is *pius* takes his responsibilities seriously and carries out all the duties of his various relationships—to the Gods, to family, to friends, and to society. Virgil was to make it *the* characteristic of Aeneas in his *Aeneid*.

LXXVII

This must be the Rufus of LXIX. The tone resembles the bitter disillusion of LXXIII and there is a similar frequency of elision. In lines 3–6 *misero*, *eripuisti*, *pestis*, *subrepsti* are echoed from LXXVI. 19–21.

4 'all I value': literally 'all our good things', cf. LXVIII. 158.

LXXVIII

One is reminded of LXXIV; perhaps Gellius is the *lepidus filius* here.

LXXVIII B

The second half of an epigram whose beginning is lost, so the prophecy of lines 3–4 has not been fulfilled.

LXXIX

Having learnt from Apuleius that Lesbia is Clodia (see Introduction, p. xix) we can deduce that this punning epigram attacks her brother Publius Clodius Pulcher, whom Cicero in a letter to Atticus refers to as *pulchellus puer* 'pretty boy' and whom in the *Pro Caelio* and elsewhere he accuses of incest with his sister.

LXXX

For Gellius see note on LXXIV. About Victor nothing is known.

LXXXI

For Juventius see note on XXIV. Pisaurum is the modern Pesaro on the Adriatic, south of Rimini.

6 *quod facinus facias*: 'what a crime you are committing', cf. CX. 4 *facis facinus*. But the present translation (perhaps wrongly) assumes a double meaning; *facinus* can be used of a person and perhaps *facere* could have the slang meaning of our 'make'.

LXXXII

A Quintius re-appears in C and a Quintia, perhaps his sister, in LXXXVI. Presumably the reference in this epigram is to Lesbia.

LXXXIII

'There is a good Freudian point here; when we speak with unnecessary fervour we are really unconvinced and trying to convince ourselves' (Ferguson). If Lesbia was Clodia Metelli, then this epigram was written before the death of Metellus in 59 B.C.

6 *loquitur*: perhaps puns on *liquitur*, 'melts', or *coquitur*, 'is cooked'.

LXXXIV

Arrius is likely to be the Quintus Arrius described by Cicero (*Brutus* 242) as an orator of low birth who without any training or natural ability made his way to high office and influence by hard work and by cultivating the right people. He was a henchman of Crassus, so that his going to Syria probably coincides with Crassus' ill-fated expedition against Parthia which left Rome late in 55 B.C.

12 *Hionios*: would possibly suggest the Greek word *chioneous* 'snowy' (so Ernest Harrison in *Classical Review* 29 (1915), 198).

LXXXV

This famous epigram disproves the theory that every good poem provides all the information needed to understand it. Presented with it out of context one could not possibly know that Catullus was talking about hating and loving the same woman at the same time. In other words we need to have read

LXXII, LXXV, and LXXVI in order to understand it. The antithesis between active *faciam* and passive *fieri* cannot be made so clear in English, whereas that between 'know' and 'feel' comes out well.

LXXXVI

For Quintia see note on LXXXII. There is the same difficulty here as in III. 1–2, to make the connection in English between *uenustas* (3) and *ueneres* (6). The last line could also be translated 'She has robbed all the Venuses of all their charms', understanding *Veneribus* (from *ueneres*) with *omnibus*.

LXXXVII

This is the first time that Catullus explicitly compares his relationship with Lesbia to a *foedus* or contract—a contract which he has faithfully kept, whereas she has not. But he has already used the word at LXIV. 335 and 373 of the marriage of Peleus and Thetis. The change in the second couplet from third to second person is emotionally effective.

LXXXVIII

The objectionable Gellius re-appears from LXXX and is now given the exceptional distinction of being the target of four consecutive epigrams. The reason for this special treatment appears in the last of them: he had betrayed Catullus' friendship by carrying on with Lesbia.

XCI

For the violent elisions in line 2 cf. LXXIII. 6 and note.

XCII

A development of LXXXIII. Despite the nadir represented by LXXVI and LXXXV, from the reader's point of view things now look brighter between Catullus and Lesbia.

XCIII

Quintilian (*Institutio Oratoria* XI. i. 38) quotes this epigram from memory: 'One of the poets says he doesn't much care whether Caesar is a black man or a white. Sheer madness. But suppose Caesar had said the same about him, then it would be arrogance.' Not to know whether someone is black or white is proverbial in Latin for complete ignorance of him.

XCIV

Mentula is Mamurra, Caesar's chief engineer, first because he is so called at XXIX. 13, and secondly because he is attacked immediately after Caesar, cf. the joint attack in LVII. It is difficult to think of an English proverb to match the Latin one here, which literally means 'Pot itself picks vegetables.'

XCV

For this epigram see Introduction, p. xxiii. In line 3 the name Hortensius may be corrupt; Catullus is his friend in LXV.

5–6 Probably quote from or allude to Cinna's own words. The Satrachus was a river in Cyprus where the story took place.

7 The Padua was a branch of the Po. For Volusius' *Annals* see XXXVI.

10 Antimachus of Colophon in Lydia was a fifth-century Greek poet admired by Plato but criticized by Callimachus who described his *Lyde* as 'fat writing and not lucid'.

XCVI

Calvus had written an elegy on the death of Quintilia, his wife or mistress. One complete pentameter survives:

Forsitan hoc etiam gaudeat ipsa cinis

which could mean 'Perhaps her very ashes may even be glad of this' or 'Perhaps herself as ashes may even be glad of this.' Catullus, in this noble epigram which is carefully structured as one marmoreal sentence, appears to be answering *forsitan . . . gaudeat* with *certe . . . gaudet*.

XCVII

The contrast with XCVI is shocking, but Catullus seems to like such gross effects; the contrast between XXXIII and XXXIV is just as violent. Line 12 pairs the epigram with XCVIII because of line 4 there. Aemilius and Victius (if the name is right) are otherwise unknown.

7 *in aestu*: perhaps 'when on heat'.

XCVIII

5 'lose us all altogether': better, perhaps, 'destroy us all completely.'

XCIX

Juventius playing up; contrast XLVIII. This is the next longest of the elegiac epigrams after LXXVI.

C

Quintius re-appears from LXXXII, Caelius from LVIII. *unica amicitia* (6) reminds the reader of LXXIII. 6 *unicum amicum* and suggests that Catullus is being ironical here. Similarly *uesana* (7) reminds of VII. 10 *uesano . . . Catullo*, and *torreret* (7) of LXVIII. 52 *torruerit*, both in a context to do with Lesbia. For *potens in* + ablative (8), 'capable of', see *Oxford Latin Dictionary* s.v. 3.

CI

A development of the sepulchral epigram, of which Book VII of the *Greek Anthology* offers many examples. 'Unlike most of these, Catullus' poem is not an epitaph. Here as elsewhere he has turned a recognized literary form into something more intimate and personal. . . . The alliteration on *m* which runs through the poem is a piece of studied technique' (Fordyce). The reader will remember from LXV and LXVIII that Catullus' brother died and was buried in the Troad. We can guess that Catullus visited the grave on his way to Bithynia (see Introduction, p. xviii).

CII

The point of this epigram is obscure and the Cornelius addressed unknown. Cornelius Nepos of I? The Cornelius of LXVII. 35? Quinn paraphrases 'Don't worry, Cornelius; I can keep a secret'. For Harpocrates see note on LXXIV.

CIII

Ten *sestertia* are ten thousand sesterces, the sum mentioned in XLI. 2. We learn from Neudling that Silo 'is an old and well-documented Italian cognomen frequently found in the inscriptions of respectable Roman citizens'. So *leno* here is likely to be mud-slinging; the word's connection with *lenis* 'gentle' gives point to the last line.

CIV

'My life' is presumably Lesbia, cf. CIX. 1; and for the second line here cf. LXXXII. It is most unusual for the addressee of an epigram to be anonymous. The name Tappo occurs in inscriptions in north Italy and in Livy as a cognomen of Valerii. *omnia monstra facis* might also mean 'you exaggerate everything', literally 'you make everything a monstrosity'.

CV

Pipla was a place and a spring on the northern side of Mt. Olympus associated with Orpheus and the Muses. Mamurra (= Mentula, cf. XCIV) must have written some verse. *furca* can be part of the human body as 'fork' in English; *scandere* can be used like 'mount' of animal copulation. It is hard to suggest this obscene double meaning in translation.

CVI

Perhaps the 'pretty boy' is Juventius—or Clodius (see note on LXXIX). Otherwise this is the only non-personal epigram in Catullus; the type is fairly common in Martial.

CVII

'A jubilant outburst after a reconciliation with Lesbia, in which excitement struggles with the restraint of form and language and the artifice of verbal repetition runs riot' (Fordyce).

> 6 'of luckier mark': literally 'of whiter mark'. 'The white mark for a lucky day . . . probably goes back to the practice of marking lucky days on a primitive calendar, and so has a similar origin to our "red-letter day" ' (Fordyce).

CVIII

Cominius is perhaps the Publius Cominius who prosecuted Publius Cornelius, a popular tribune of the plebs, in the mid 60s B.C., thereby incurring their hatred. His dismemberment here by birds and beasts has a parallel in the *Ibis* of Ovid, which may suggest a common source in Callimachus' famous poem of that name.

CIX

The change from second to third person here is the reverse of that in LXXXVII. In this final appearance of Lesbia we find her at last offering Catullus the sort of love he has longed for, and Catullus himself praying that the Gods will keep her up to the mark. The idea of marriage as friendship appears to be Catullus' own. 'The *foedus*', Lyne writes, 'is to be maintained *tota uita*; if Catullus calls Lesbia *mea uita* in that context, it is a simple and eloquent statement of where he stands.'

CX

Aufillena, introduced in C, re-appears in this and the next epigram. She comes as a surprise after Lesbia in CIX. Does the *sanctae foedus amicitiae* allow Catullus to have a bit on the side? Or is that unfair and does this placing imply that Lesbia failed him once more?

> 3–4 Or 'You, because you unfriendly broke your promise to me,/Because you don't give but often take, commit a crime'.

> 7 Text uncertain.

CXI

'The poet manages to cap the charge made in CX' (Goold).

   4 *fratres*: = *fratres patrueles* 'cousins'; *patruus* is 'father's brother', cf. LXXIV.

CXII

The identity of Naso is unknown. The epigram puns on *multus homo* = 'a busybody' and 'many a person'.   'Wish to know you': literally 'go down with you', sc. 'to the Forum' for business, but also preparing for *pathicus*.   A Martial-type epigram.

CXIII

Maecilia is a perfectly good Roman name, but we know nothing else about her. Pompey was consul in 70 B.C. and again in 55, which makes this one of the datable epigrams.

CXIV and CXV

These two strange epigrams about Mamurra and his estate at Firmum (on the coast south of Ancona) contain textual difficulties but their general sense is clear. 'Mamurra's extravagant habits and the words of Catullus make it probable that this *saltus* was used for sport rather than profit' (Munro).

CXVI

Carmina . . . Battiadae (2) echoes the same two words in LXV. 16, thus rounding off the third book of Catullus' poems. He returns to Gellius (6) from the group of four epigrams LXXXVIII–XCI. Again there is textual difficulty—not however with lines 3 and 8, both of which offer features unparalleled elsewhere in Catullus. Line 3 is a totally spondaic line, and line 8 elides final *s* before a consonant (admittedly another *s*), a thing which Cicero labels *subrusticum* 'countrified', and says is avoided by 'modern poets' (nevertheless Catullus writes *ultu' peccatum* at XLIV. 17, if Muretus's emendation is accepted). Wiseman (1985, 184–9) offers an attractive explanation. He identifies our Catullus with a Catullus known to have written mimes. He points out that the spondaic hexameter can equally well be read as a spondaic iambic senarius (and the iambic senarius is the metre used in mime). According to him Catullus is giving crafty notice of his intention to say goodbye to the erudite manner of Callimachus and take up the laxer style befitting his new genre—the mime.

APPENDIX A
Differences from Mynors's Oxford Classical Text (1985 reprint)

(The O.C.T. reading is given second. Minor differences of spelling, capitalization, punctuation, etc. are not recorded.)

IV. 8   Thracia *Thomson*: Thraciam
24 nouissime *V*: nouissimo

VI. 12 nam nil ista ualet *Lachmann*: †nam inista preualet†
13 cum *Camps*: cur?

IX. 2 antestans *Palladius*: antistans

X. 10 nunc *Westphal*: nec

XI. 11 horribiles uitro *McKie*: horribile aequor

XIV. 16 salse *G*: false

XXI. 3 antehac (*or* antea) *Translator*: aut sunt
11 a temet *Froehlich*: me met

XXII. 5 palimpsesto *V*: palimpseston
13 tritius *Pontanus*: scitius

XXIII. 21 lupillis *Gulielmus*: lapillis
23 possis *pre-1460*: posses

XXV. 5 miluorum aues *Palmer*: †mulier aries†
11 conscribilent flagella *Turnebus*: flagella conscribillent

XXIX. 20 et huicne Gallia et metet Britannia? *Munro*: nunc Galliae timetur et Britanniae
23 urbis o piissimi *Haupt*: †urbis opulentissimi†

XXX. 5 quod *Mueller*: quae

XXXVII. 5 putere *Hermann*: putare

XXXIX. 11 parcus *V*: pinguis

XLII 13 facit. *Halbertsma*: facis?
14 potest *c.1430*: potes

XLIV. 17 ultu' *Muretus*: ulta.

LI. 8 ⟨uocis in ore⟩ *Ritter*: . . .

LIV. 2 et, trirustice, *Munro*: †et erit rustice
5 Fuficio *Scaliger*: Sufficio

LV. 3 te in *Sillig*: te
9 a, cette huc *Camps*: †aueltet
uoque *Muretus*: ipse
11 'en' inquit quaedam *Gould*. quaedam inquit
sinum reducens *Avantius*: nudum reduc . . .

LVIII B. 10 mi amice *Scaliger*: mihi, amice

LXI. 77 ades *Schrader*: adest
216 obuiis *Pleitner*: omnibus

LXIII. 78 and 83 Ferox *Translator*: ferox
85 rabidum *Schwabe*: rapidum
animum *Baehrens*: animo

LXIV. 11 prora *O*: prima
14 feri *V*: freti
23b iter⟨um mihi formosarum⟩ *Translator*: iter⟨um . . .
89 progignunt *pre-1468*: praecingunt
104 succendit *V*: succepit
119 lamentatast *Conington*: laeta⟨batur⟩
140 miseram *1472*: miserae
148 meminere *Czwalina*: metuere
164 conqueror *pre-1452*: conquerar
174 in Creta *O*: in Cretam
178 a *V*: at
179 truculentum ubi *V*: truculentum

243 inflati *V*: infecti
254 cui Thyades *Skutsch*: quae tum alacres *with
        lacuna after 253*
276 uestibulo *Schrader*: uestibuli
287 Haemonisin *Heinsius*: †Minosim
        Dryasin *Translator*: †doris
320 uellentes *Fruter*: pellentes
351 putriaque *Heinsius*: putridaque
387 residens *Baehrens*: reuisens
395 Amarynthia *Baehrens*: Amarunsia
402 uti nuptae *Maehly*: ut innuptae
        nouellae *Baehrens*: nouercac

LXV. 9 *supplied by Palmer*: . . . . .

LXVI. 7 limine *Heinsius*: lumine
        9 cunctis . . . deorum *Haupt*: multis . . . dearum
       21 an *15th century*: et
       30 tersti *Avantius*: tristi
       59 hic liquidi *Friedrich*: †hi dii uen ibi†
           limine *pre-1468*: lumine
       63 fletu *15th century*: fluctu
       74 uere *V*: ueri
       77 quidem erat muliebribus *Skutsch*: quondam fuit
           omnibus
       92 effice *V*: affice
       93 cur iterent *V*: corruerint   .

LXVII. 12 uere, etsi populi uana loquela *Translator*: uerum
           †istius populi ianua qui te†
        20 attigerat *pre-1460*: attigerit
        37 qui *1502*: quid?

LXVIII. 11 and 30 Manli *1457*: Mani
         139 contudit *Herzberg*: concoquit
         141 Between this and 142 Mynors marks a lacuna of
             two verses
         148 diem *1473*: dies
         156 in qua nos *15th century*: ⟨ipsa⟩ in qua
         157 te tradidit *Scaliger*, Afer *Munro*: †terram dedit
             aufert†
         158 primo mi omnia *Haupt*: primo omnia

LXXI. 4 apte *pre-1479*: †a te

LXXVI. 3 in ullo *pre-1468*: nullo
 11 animum *Statius*: animo

LXXVII. 5 and 6 eheu *Baehrens*: heu heu

LXXXVII. 3 umquam in *Palladius*: umquam

XCV. 9 sunt *15th century*: sint
 ⟨sodalis⟩ *1502*: . . .

XCVII. 5 os *Froehlich*: hoc

XCIX. 8 abstersti *O*: abstersisti
 mollibus *Translator*: omnibus
 15 amanti *Translator*: amori

C. 6 est igni tum *Palmer*: ex igni est

CI. 4 cinerem, *and* 6 mihi. *many editors*: cinerem.
 and mihi,

CII. 1 quoiquam tacitum *Statius*: quicquam tacito

CVII. 3 nobis quoque—*Munro*: †nobis quoque†
 7 hac re *Kroll*: †hac est
 8 optandum in *Ellis*: †optandus

CX. 7 est furis *Munro*: officiis . . . est

CXI. 4 ⟨parere⟩ *Doering*: . . .

CXII. 1 ⟨est qui⟩ *Scaliger*: ⟨est quin⟩
 2 descendit *V*: te scindat

CXV. 1 iuxta *Scaliger*: instar
 5 uastasque paludes *Pleitner*: saltusque paludesque

CXVI. 2 uertere *Palmer*: mittere
 7 euitamus amictu *c.1450*: euitabimus †amitha

APPENDIX B
The Metres of Catullus
(in the order of their appearance)

1. *Hendecasyllables*

This is Catullus' name for the line of eleven syllables that he uses in no less than forty of the Epigrams I–LX. The first line of his *libellus* represents its most usual form, opening with a spondee, i.e. two long syllables; the last syllable of the line in this and the other metres he uses can be indifferently long or short:

> *Cūi dō|nō lĕpĭdūm|nŏuŭm|lĭbēllūm?*

Occasionally (for the details see Introduction, p. xxi) the initial spondee is replaced by a trochee (–∪) as in I. 2 or an iamb (∪–) as in I. 4. In LV and LVIII B he combines the hendecasyllabic with a decasyllabic line in which the two consecutive short syllables of the hendecasyllabic are replaced by one long syllable, as in LVIII B. 1:

> *Nōn cūs|tōs sī fīn|găr īl|lĕ Crētūm.*

2. *Iambic trimeter, or senarius*

A *metron* here consists of two iambs (∪–∪–), and the line consists of three *metra* (hence trimeter) or six iambs (hence the Latin name *senarius*). Catullus uses the pure form of this metre twice, in IV and XXIX:

> *Phăsēlŭs īl|lĕ quēm uĭdē|tĭs, hōspĭtēs,*

and

> *Quĭs hōc pŏtēst|uĭdērĕ, quĭs|pŏtēst pătī?*

In LII. 2 and 3 he allows spondees to replace the odd-numbered iambs, thus:

> *pēr cōnsŭlā|tūm pēiĕrāt|Vātīnĭŭs.*

3. *Scazons, or choliambics*

The word means 'limping iambics' and the line is an iambic trimeter ending with a spondee (or trochee):

> Mĭsēr Cătūl|lĕ, dēsĭnās|ĭnēptīrĕ.

Catullus uses the metre eight times, in VIII, XXII, XXXI, XXXVII, XXXIX, XLIV, LIX, and LX. The first and the third short syllables are sometimes long.

4. *Sapphics*

The Sapphic stanza is used in XI and LI. Its pattern is:

$$- \cup - \underset{\smile}{-} \ - \cup \cup - \cup - \underset{\smile}{-} \quad \text{(lines 1–3)}$$
$$- \cup \cup - \underset{\smile}{-} \quad \text{(line 4)}$$

5. *Priapeans*

This line of fifteen syllables, which Catullus uses once only, in XVII, consists of a glyconic (eight syllables) plus a pherecratean (seven syllables):

> O Cŏ|lōnĭă quāe|cŭpīs||pōntĕ|lūdĕrĕ lōn|gō.

The second syllable of each is sometimes long.

6. *Iambic tetrameter catalectic, or septenarius*

Used in XXV only and so called because the fourth iambic metron is incomplete:

> Cĭnāēdĕ Thāl|lĕ, mōllĭōr|cŭnīcŭlī|căpīllō.

The Latin name implies that the line consists of seven iambs (plus an overspill). First and fifth short syllables are sometimes long.

7. *Greater Asclepiad*

Used in XXX only, this line is basically a glyconic (see 5 above) with two extra choriambs (– ∪ ∪ –) inserted in it:

iām tē|nīl mĭsĕrēt,|dūrĕ, tŭī|dūlcīs ămī|cŭlī?

8. *Glyconic strophes*

In Catullus these consist of either three (XXXIV) or four (LXI) glyconics plus a pherecratean (see 5 above).

9. *Dactylic hexameter*

Catullus uses this well-known metre in LXII and LXIV. Basically it consists of five dactyls (‒ ∪ ∪) plus a spondee (or trochee); any or all of the first four dactyls may be replaced by a spondee. In LXIV Catullus is fond of replacing the fifth dactyl with a spondee, producing what is called a spondaic hexameter or *spondeiazon*, e.g. LXIV. 3:

Phāsĭdŏs|ād flūc|tūs ēt|fīnēs|Āeē|tēōs.

10. *Galliambics*

This metre, used in LXIII, owes its name to its connection with the worship of Cybele, whose priests were known as *Galli*. LXIII. 1 shows the commonest form of the line, which always falls into two halves:

Sŭpĕr āltă uēc|tŭs Āttīs||cĕlĕrī rătĕ mă|rĭă.

By the substitution of one long syllable for two short the line can be compressed into its shortest form, as in LXIII. 73:

iām ıām dŏlēt|quŏd ēgī,||ıam ıāmquĕ paē|nĭtĕt.

The commonest form of the line demands ten short syllables, four of them consecutive, and must have been difficult to handle in Latin, where long syllables are commoner. Even so, very occasionally, Catullus resolves a long syllable into two short, as at line 91:

Dĕă, māgnă Dĕă,|Cўbēbē,||Dĕă Dŏmĭnă Dīn|dўmī.

11. *Elegiac couplet*

This, the commonest metre in Catullus, is used from LXV onwards to the end of the whole collection. It consists of a dactylic hexameter (see 9 above) plus a pentameter. The pentameter can be thought of as a hexameter with one long syllable missing in the middle and one at the end, thus:

$$- \cup \bar{\cup} | - \cup \bar{\cup} | - || - \cup \cup | - \cup \cup | \underset{\smile}{\bar{}}$$

But its second half must always contain two dactyls. Catullus treats the metre in the Greek fashion, often ending the line with words of more than two syllables and sometimes using elision between the two halves.

SELECT BIBLIOGRAPHY

Editions and Commentaries

BAEHRENS, E. (1885). *Catulli Veronensis Liber*, Leipzig. A Latin commentary on the text he published in 1876.

ELLIS, R. (1889). *A Commentary on Catullus*, 2nd edn., Oxford.

—— (1904). *Catulli Carmina*, Oxford.

FORDYCE, C. J. (1961). *Catullus: a Commentary*, Oxford. Includes the Latin (Oxford Text) but omits 32 poems.

GOOLD, G. P. (1983). *Catullus, edited with introduction, translation, and notes*, London.

KROLL, W. (1922). *C. Valerius Catullus, herausgegeben und erklärt*, Stuttgart (5th reprint, with addenda, 1968).

MERRILL, E. T. (1893). *Catullus, edited with commentary and critical appendix*, Cambridge, Mass. (reprinted 1951).

MYNORS, R. A. B. (1958). *C. Valerii Catulli Carmina*, Oxford.

PALMER, A. (1896). *Catulli Veronensis Liber*, London.

POSTGATE, J. P. (1889). *Gai Valeri Catulli Carmina*, London.

QUINN, K. (1970). *Catullus, the poems*, London.

THOMSON, D. F. S. (1978). *Catullus, a critical edition*, Chapel Hill.

Translations

CORNISH, F. W. (1913). *The Poems of Gaius Valerius Catullus*, London. Loeb Classical Library, with Latin text (2nd edition, revised by G. P. Goold, 1988).

GOOLD, G. P. (1983). See section above.

RAPHAEL, F. and MCLEISH, K. (1978). *The Poems of Catullus*, London.

WHIGHAM, P. (1966). *The Poems of Catullus*, Penguin Books, London.

Studies

CAIRNS, F. (1974). 'Venusta Sirmio', in *Quality and Pleasure in Latin Poetry*, ed. A. J. Woodman and D. A. West, Cambridge, 1–17.

—— (1975). 'Catullus 27', *Mnemosyne* 28, 24–9.

CLAUSEN, W. V. (1982). 'The New Direction in Poetry', in *The Cambridge History of Classical Literature* II. 178–206.

FERGUSON, J. (1985). *Catullus*, Lawrence, Kansas. Discusses each poem.

—— (1988). *Catullus* (*Greece & Rome*: New Surveys in the Classics, No. 20), Oxford.

FRAENKEL, E. (1955). 'VESPER ADEST', *Journal of Roman Studies* 45, 1–8.

HARRAUER, H. (1977). *A Bibliography to Catullus*, Hildesheim.

LYNE, R. O. A. M. (1980). *The Latin Love Poets, from Catullus to Horace*, Oxford, 19–61.

MUNRO, H. A. J. (1905). *Criticisms and Elucidations of Catullus*, 2nd edn., London.

NEUDLING, C. L. (1955). *A Prosopography to Catullus*, Oxford.

QUINN, K. (1969). *The Catullan Revolution*, revised impression, Cambridge.

—— (1972). *Catullus: an interpretation*, London.

—— ed. (1972). *Approaches to Catullus*, Cambridge.

SKUTSCH, O. (1969). 'Metrical Variations and Some Textual Problems in Catullus', *Bulletin of the Institute of Classical Studies* 16, 38–43.

SMALL, S. G. P. (1983). *Catullus: a reader's guide to the poems*, New York.

WETMORE, M. N. (1912). *Index Verborum Catullianus*, New Haven, Connecticut (reprinted Hildesheim, 1961).

WISEMAN, T. P. (1969). *Catullan Questions*, Leicester.

—— (1985). *Catullus and his World*, Cambridge.

The Oxford World's Classics Website

www.worldsclassics.co.uk

- Information about new titles
- Explore the full range of Oxford World's Classics
- Links to other literary sites and the main OUP webpage
- Imaginative competitions, with bookish prizes
- Peruse the Oxford World's Classics Magazine
- Articles by editors
- Extracts from Introductions
- A forum for discussion and feedback on the series
- Special information for teachers and lecturers

www.worldsclassics.co.uk